Now Mr Editor!

Letters to the Newspapers of Nineteenth Century Birmingham

Stephen Roberts

Published under the imprint *Birmingham Biographies*

Printed by CreateSpace

ISBN-13: 978-1518685897

ISBN-10: 1518685897

Front cover: A caricature of Jonathan Crowther, editor of the *Birmingham Journal* from 1829 until 1833. He is depicted in an inebriated state outside Henry Cattell's Bell Inn.

REWRITING THE BOOK
THE LIBRARY OF BIRMINGHAM

For Jerry Fenwick

Contents

Acknowledgements

𝔉ive of the illustrations in this book are reproduced by kind permission of the Birmingham and Midland Institute and and three of the illustrations are reproduced with the permission of the Library of Birmingham. I wish to thank the staff of both institutions for the assistance they gave me during my visits.

I am grateful to Carl Chinn, William Dargue, Ian Haywood and Sue Thomas for responding to my queries; to Roger Ward for providing me with a copy of his article on Joseph Allday; and to Richard Brown for his comments on part of this book and for his technical expertise.

And, finally, thanks also to Felix Mendelssohn whose magnificent oratorio 'Elijah' - first performed in the town hall in Birmingham in August 1846 – provided very appropriate musical accompaniment during the long hours it took to transcribe the letters which appear in this book.

Foreword

⊤he ultra-Tory satirical journal the *Monthly Argus and Public Censor*, edited by local iron monger Joseph Allday, was scathing about the newspapers of early nineteenth century Birmingham:

It is somewhat curious that, at this moment, Birmingham is more lamentably deficient in anything like a respectable newspaper press than any other town in the kingdom. Places which may be accounted villages – when compared with the immense extent, wealth and importance of Birmingham – can boast of a press more talented and independent than belongs to the Boeotia of England ...[1]

Aris's Birmingham Gazette – established 1741 – was once considered one of the best paying local papers in England. We believe it ranked with the *Leeds Mercury* (which may be called the provincial *Times*) and, as a source of profit, was considered to hold its head very lofty above its provincial compeers. As an organ of political opinion, it never was esteemed. It felt that its strength lay in its profits, and it did not spare a line which could be devoted to the services of its advertising friends. It was always anything but a paper of news ... its columns are too much crowded with advertisements.

The *Birmingham Journal* .... is now become such a sink of bigotry, twaddle, ignorance, lies, sedition and whatever is disgraceful to humanity that no barely decent or honest man can peruse it without having his moral feelings outraged to an insufferable degree ... I ask, in the name of common sense and common honesty, how much longer the people of Birmingham intend to tolerate the bare-faced humbug, quackery and infamous one-sided policy of the factious *Journal?*[2]

---

[1] Boeotia was a region of ancient Greece, located north-west of Athens.

[2] *Monthly Argus and Public Censor,* I, pp. 558-9; IV, p. 171; V, p. 160. Joseph Allday manufactured and sold at Dale End such items as fenders, cutlery, teapots and bird cages: see advertisement in *Aris's Birmingham Gazette,* 29 January 1827. He was declared bankrupt in summer 1829. His vituperative journal could only be obtained from its publisher William Chidlow of Great Charles Street. On several occasions articles in the *Monthly Argus* led to writs being issued for libel. Allday was later an influential figure on the town council, as leader of a group known as the economists.

So Allday disliked one of the two principal papers published in his town, and loathed the other. There was one other paper, with a far smaller circulation, that managed to keep going, the *Birmingham Advertiser*, which survived from October 1833 until November 1844; but other attempts to bring out a successful weekly failed. In 1829, for example, the *Birmingham and Coventry Free Press* – also 'a filthy, flimsy sheet', in Allday's view – managing to sell only 400 copies of each issue and survived for only six weeks whilst plans to launch the *Birmingham Independent* came to nothing.[3] *Aris's Gazette* had been published continuously in Birmingham since November 1740, the first issue containing just five lines of local news and two local advertisements. The paper took its name from its proprietor Thomas Aris, a London-born bookseller and stationer located in New Street. By the time that Allday was writing, the main shareholders in the paper were Paul Moon James, the manager of the Birmingham Banking Company and later High Bailiff, R.W. Gem, a solicitor and magistrate, William Pare, an importer of snuff and cigars and Thomas Smith. Though Thomas Knott had been in place as editor since 1814, it was widely believed that it was James, a published poet, who wrote many of the leading articles whilst Pare contributed the reports of public meetings. In the late 1820s these men faced a falling circulation: sales stood at little more than 1,800 a week, having declined from almost 5,000 a week some years earlier.

Though the *Gazette* could be relied upon to support Toryism and Protestantism, it was not a full-blooded enough publication for the Birmingham Tories. Meeting at their favourite haunt, Joe Linden's 'Minerva', in 1825 local Tories decided to launch a rival newspaper.[4] The first issue was edited by a Unitarian called Bakewell, and printed by William Hodgetts of Spiceal Street. The son of a Deritend iron founder, Hodgetts had been apprenticed to Miles Swinney, a printer in the High Street, before setting himself up on his own account in his mid-twenties; at his shop he also sold

---

[3] *Monthly Argus and Public Censor,* I, p. 561. To stay afloat a newspaper needed to sell in the high hundreds, as the *Advertiser* did. A number of literary and theatrical monthlies, most of them short-lived, were also published in Birmingham at this time e.g. the *Looker-On.*

[4] The circumstances in which the newspaper came into being were recounted in Eliezer Edwards' 'First Impressions of Birmingham', which forms the introduction to this book.

books and quack medicines. At first editorials for the *Journal* were supplied by a London journalist, but after a time Bakewell began to write them himself. Allday was unimpressed: 'Mr Bakewell ... although a very good reporter was, without doubt, one of the most milk-and-watery scribes the world ever saw ... he never seemed to enter warmly or sincerely into advocacy or assertion of Protestantism'.[5] It was not uncommon for the often incautious journalists of the 1820s to find themselves embroiled in libel cases. When such an action was successfully pursued against the *Journal* at the Gloucester Assizes in autumn 1826, it was the beginning of the end for the main shareholders; with a bill to meet of £1600, they passed the entire paper on to Hodgetts for a sum of little more than £400.

Hodgetts was actually looking to sell the paper at a profit, but sales began to increase (from 750 a week in 1828 to 1250 in 1830) and he was to remain proprietor until September 1833. Bakewell did not long survive the change in ownership, buying his own periodical in Somerset. The new editor was R. Shelton Mackenzie, who, at the height of agitation for Catholic emancipation, made the editorial line of the paper avowedly Protestant. 'From a lukewarm system of comments on the Pasha of Egypt (the only point in foreign politics ever alluded to by the former editor) and from a fearful and aloetic glancing at local abuses', Allday wrote approvingly, 'the *Birmingham Journal* suddenly started and spoke of politics, local, domestic and foreign, in a style to which provincial journals had heretofore been unaccustomed.'[6] Hodgetts' new man, however, was gone within a year, leaving to take up a better offer as editor of the *Carlisle Patriot*. At the end of 1829, Jonathan Crowther arrived from Warrington to become editor. Another printer and bookseller who moved into journalism, Crowther had worked as a reporter for the *Manchester Courier and Lancashire General Advertiser*. It was alleged by Allday that, in these early days, Crowther was assisted in writing the content of the paper by George Edmonds, a one-time Particular Baptist who, in 1819-20, had brought out a series of short-lived radical journals:

---

5 *Monthly Argus and Public Censor,* I, pp. 559-60.
6 *Monthly Argus and Public Censor,* I, p. 200.

'When Crowther, redolent of pipe and pot,
In every line displays himself a sot,
Whether his leading articles he brings
From George Edmonds, in his leading strings,
(For his own leaden articles we see
Fill but some half-dozen lines of idiocy);
Or sneer at things that better men have done,
This ballad-printing hack from Warrington'[7]

Edmonds denied that he was involved and the acrimonious
relationship between the two men eventually resulted in the issuing
of writs for libel. For Crowther the abuse showed no signs of
relenting:

'Cease, rude drunkard, cease your snoring,
Place your hat straight on your head,
Don't you feel the rain is pouring;
Or are all your senses dead?
Hark! Jonathan, the watchman's bawling;
Hark! He cries out at half past two.
Is this the respect you show, sir,
To the *Journal* good and true?
Still I fain would you know, sir,
I don't doubt you're pink and blue'[8]

Astutely catching the political wind in Birmingham, Hodgetts
and Crowther decided to throw the paper's support behind the
cause of parliamentary reform. The Political Union, founded in
January 1830, began to put in orders for 200 copies whenever its
meetings were reported. In Hodgetts' obituary, it was recorded that
in these excited months 'his doors were besieged by anxious crowds
struggling to secure early copies'.[9] In September 1832 Hodgetts was

---

[7] *Birmingham in 1830: A Satirical Poem,* reviewed in *Monthly Argus and Public
Censor,* II, p. 550. *Edmunds's Weekly Recorder,* June-August 1819; *Edmonds'
Weekly Register,* August 1819-January 1820; *Edmonds's Birmingham Gazette,*
September 1819; *Saturday Register,* January-March 1820.
[8] *Monthly Argus and Public Censor,* V, p. 124. To accuse a political opponent of
being a drunkard was a common insult in this period; according to Allday,
Crowther would sit in the Bell public house on the Bristol Road, boasting of
saving the *Birmingham Journal.* Political colours were localized at this time,
with, in Birmingham, pink and blue representing the Liberal cause.
[9] *Birmingham Daily Post,* 3 January 1874.

able to sell the *Journal* to the reform party for £2000, a handsome profit.[10] The leading figures in these new arrangements were R.S. Rintoul, the editor of the *Spectator*, and, locally, the solicitor and election agent Joseph Parkes. Crowther went with Hodgetts to the newly established *Birmingham Advertiser* and was succeeded as editor of the *Journal* by R.K. Douglas. The paper remained committed to a reform programme – promoting, according to Allday's *Advertiser*, 'a nauseous toadyism of the Scholefields' - and, in 1837, had an average circulation of 2,115.[11] It sold by Parkes to the Sligo-born journalist John Frederick Feeney in 1844.

The *Gazette* had meanwhile become the paper for the gentlemen of Birmingham who found themselves out of sympathy with reform and cared most of all for the defence of property and of Protestantism. Throughout the nineteenth century Toryism in Birmingham was always a minority cause, but never a silent one. The paper that championed the Tory cause in fact outsold its liberal rival by some margin, boasting an average circulation of 3,153 in 1837. Though the principal shareholder P.M. James left Birmingham in 1836 to become manager of the Manchester and Salford Joint Stock Bank, R. W. Gem remained and was joined by his son and two new major shareholders. There were not the upheavals at the *Gazette* that characterised the *Journal*. Thomas Knott - by all accounts a modest and kind-hearted man – served as editor for twenty five years until, in July 1839, he died suddenly as the result of a stroke.[12] His successor, a reporter called Cooper, did not last anything like as long, being dismissed in November 1840 (for which he was subsequently awarded £200 in damages); but thereafter business continued in its usual stately pace. 'Mrs Aris' -

---

[10] In his later years Hodgetts devoted himself to bringing out religious publications. Crowther later became a correspondent for *The Times* and died in December 1859.

[11] *Birmingham Journal*, 17 November 1838. For its part the editor of the *Journal* branded the men behind the *Advertiser* as 'false and infamous libellers' and claimed the paper was on the verge of bankruptcy (ibid., 11 November, 17 November 1837). A banker, Joshua Scholefield became deputy chairman of the Birmingham Political Union and, in 1832, was returned, with Thomas Attwood, as one of the MPs for the town; William Scholefield, his second son, was, in 1838-9, the first Mayor of Birmingham and, from 1844, also represented the town in Parliament.

[12] *Aris's Gazette*, 15 July 1839.

as the paper was affectionately known in the town - was to remain 'a paper of great provincial celebrity'.[13]

The town's two newspapers appeared on different days, the *Gazette* on a Monday morning and the *Journal* on a Saturday morning. Relations between the editors of the two publications remained cordial – on at least two occasions, in September 1834 and in July 1837, the *Journal,* after encountering technological problems, was produced on the printing machine of its rival. During its earlier years the *Journal* cost half a penny less than the *Gazette,* but, in August 1838, the price was increased so that both papers cost 5d. Profits were never high for either publication. 'W.H. says the Birmingham press is not half-worked', the editor of the *Journal* lamented in September 1842. 'If he had the working of it, we rather think he would soon find it better worked than paid. We do not believe there is an operative in the kingdom that has so much occasion to complain that he does not get "a fair day's wage for a fair day's work" as have nineteenths of the proprietors of the provincial journals of England.'[14]

This book gathers together a selection of readers' letters published in the correspondence columns of *Aris's Birmingham Gazette* and the *Birmingham Journal* between 1820 and 1850. A greater number of letters appeared in the later part of this period – but advertisements always took precedence and letters rarely numbered more than four or five. Allday claimed that the *Gazette* only published letters that concurred with the views of its editor and owners. This claim doubtless resulted from the rejection of his own offerings, but a perusal of the correspondence columns of these newspapers suggests that readers tended to write to the publication they were most in sympathy with, even if they were commenting on something they had read elsewhere – it was not unusual for a correspondent to begin a letter by referring to an item in a rival organ. The *Journal* declared that its policy was 'to admit any letter from any correspondent which is conceived in orderly and decent terms, even if it should happen to attack Mr Attwood'[15]; but those

---

[13] *Birmingham Journal,* 3 April 1841.

[14] Ibid., 3 September 1841.

[15] *Birmingham Journal,* 16 November 1839. Thomas Attwood was a figure of central importance in the town from the time of his appointment as High Bailiff in 1811 until the early 1840s, when ill health and business troubles led to his

who wished to attack Attwood, or any of the reformers, preferred to do so in the columns of the *Gazette*. (Attwood invariably replied with great vigour). Few correspondents put their names to their letters, preferring initials or pseudonyms. This certainly annoyed Thomas Clutton Salt, one of the leaders of the Political Union: 'Against a man in a mask there is no fair chance. Pray tell us why you do not hunt out of the *Journal* office these grubbing moles? It is enough to have them at *Aris's Gazette* and the *Advertiser*'[16] Of course, the correspondence which makes up the main section of this book expresses only the views of those who were capable of writing letters or were bothered to do so. This means that these are decidedly middle class, male views, but they do offer an illuminating insight into what the educated, confident section of the population of Birmingham in the first part of the nineteenth century thought about what was happening in their town. What these letters achieved in practical terms is difficult to gauge. Clearly calls to action to fellow townsmen – for example, over the setting up of a cemetery company – brought results. However, we will simply never know if the coal carts in front of the shops at Snow Hill or the inaccuracy of the clock at Christ Church were ever dealt with.[17] Most of the letters are reprinted in full, though Victorian newspaper correspondents could be prolix and so a small number have been shortened.

---

withdrawal from public life; his championing of parliamentary reform led to him being referred to as 'King Tom' by local people.

[16] Ibid.

[17] Christ Church, built between 1805 and 1815, was situated at the end of New Street, opposite the town hall. It was generally regarded by the local populace aa an ugly building and, at the end of the century, demolished.

Introduction:
Eliezer Edward's Impressions of Birmingham in 1837

*E*liezer Edwards' reminiscences of Birmingham and the men he had known, published under a pseudonym in the mid-1870s, proved to be extremely popular with the readers of the *Birmingham Daily Mail*, and so 'the well-known S.D.R.', as Walter Showell described him, revised and extended his sketches and published them as *Personal Recollections of Birmingham and Birmingham Men* in 1877.[1] This closely-printed book was divided up into fifteen chapters, eleven of them portraits of local notables – the MP G.F. Muntz, the minister Charles Vince, the pen maker Joseph Gillott and so on – but also including detailed descriptions of local banks and of the Bull Ring riots of 1839, the latter laced with hostility towards Feargus O'Connor and the Chartists. This collection was described at the time as 'very readable, alike from its pleasant style and from the gossiping, anecdotal character of its matter'.[2] This is a very apt evaluation. When I was musing on an introduction to this selection from the correspondence columns of *Aris's Birmingham Gazette* and the *Birmingham Journal* between 1820 and 1850, it occurred to me that nothing would be more suitable than an edited version of the richly-detailed first essay in Edwards' book, 'First Impressions of Birmingham'.

Edwards was not a Birmingham man. He was born in Bristol in 1815 and spent his early years in Greenwich and Rochester in Kent and in Guildford in Surrey, being twenty two years old when, in his capacity as a travelling salesman, he first visited Birmingham. On this first visit he stayed for six months. In the early 1840s Edwards was employed by the textiles wholesalers Bradbury, Greatrex & Co. in London, but, in 1845, settled permanently in Birmingham. One of his brothers was the manager at the tea merchant W. Dakin & Co in High Street, and it as in the town that

---

[1] *Showell's Dictionary of Birmingham* (1885). Walter Showell was a very wealthy brewer; his dictionary was actually compiled by local antiquarian Thomas T. Harman. Though its errors were noted at the time (see reviews in *Birmingham Daily Post*, 28 December 1885 and *Edgbastonia*, January 1886), the volume remains an essential source for all those with an interest in Victorian Birmingham.

[2] *Birmingham Daily Post*, 14 December 1877.

Edwards found his wife (a relative of the factor and magistrate Henry Van Wart.)[3] Edwards died in Birmingham, at his Harborne residence, Lindon House, in February 1891[4]

How did Edwards make a living? It certainly wasn't from journalism, which he only took up in his sixties. Edwards in fact described himself as a manufacturer, operating at 49 St. Paul's Square. In the 1850s he set himself up as a glass manufacturer. Glass knobs, handles and finger plates for doors were the main items that he manufactured, and he registered patents for improvements in the apparatus used to produce these. It was clearly a small-scale operation: Edwards himself would traipse around Birmingham, drumming up custom. Edwards also had other commercial plans, registering patents for new types of gas stove and, most remarkably, for a bedstead 'which may be used as a vehicle'.[5] An additional source of income came from acting as the agent in Birmingham for the Provident Clerks' Mutual Benefit Association and Benevolent Fund, which provided assistance in old age or to families after the death of members.[6]

What is clear is that Edwards was not a very successful businessman. In 1857 he borrowed money from the Professional and Commercial Building Society, but within a year was defaulting on repayments. Eventually the building society sought to take possession of Edward's property, but he managed to stave this off. To no one's great surprise, least of all his own, Edwards was declared bankrupt in August 1871. It was said that he 'had expended large sums of money in improving his works, but in this expenditure he had been unfortunate. The business had been carried on until it was literally exhausted'[7] Edwards owed £3,142. 16s.9d, with assets worth only £308.3s.7d.

---

[3] William Dakin opened his tea business in Birmingham in 1821 and sold it to Philpott & Son in 1840; Henry Van Wart, though an American by birth, was described as 'essentially a Birmingham man' in his obituary in the *Birmingham Daily Post*, 17 February 1873.

[4] *Birmingham Daily Post*, 23 February 1891, *Edgbastonia*, March 1891, for short obituaries, which have nothing to say about his business career.

[5] *London Gazette*, 4 February, 11 February, 30 September 1853, 17 October 1856, 10 August 1858, 24 July, 17 November 1863, 16 July, 4 November 1874.

[6] Provident Mutual Life Assurance, as this company became, was dissolved in 2003.

[7] *Birmingham Daily Post*, 31 August 1871.

It was through his pen rather than his patents that Edwards found his greatest success. *Personal Recollections* (1877) was followed by *Old Taverns of Birmingham* (1879) and *Words, Facts and Phrases* (1881), a six hundred page compendium which took three years to assemble and was pronounced as having 'a great deal of really curious learning in it'.[8] But Edwards' greatest literary success was *Edgbastonia.* Launched in May 1881, it continued long after the death of its proprietor. The highlight of each issue was Edwards' speciality – a portrait of a well-known local figure. There was no shortage of suitable subjects in Edgbaston, and Edwards ranged across politicians, ministers, physicians, artists and musicians. Within a few years 2,500 copies of the magazine were being distributed free of charge across Edgbaston. Endorsements of local businesses covered the costs (£1,500 in the first five years), but it is clear that profits were small.[9] An addict for newspapers and magazines, *Edgbastonia* was clearly a labour of love for Edwards.

It is a curiosity of late Victorian and Edwardian Birmingham that none of the prominent men – J. T. Bunce, R.W. Dale, Sir Benjamin Stone and the rest – published memoirs or reminiscences. We have Sir Richard Tangye's autobiography, but it was a reluctantly-written volume by a man who preferred not to draw attention to himself. Edwards' *Personal Recollections* stand almost alone; but anyone with an interest in Victorian Birmingham will find the volume, full of small detail and honest and frank assessments, a treat to read.

*   *   *

First Impressions of Birmingham

It is a fine autumnal morning in the year 1837. I am sitting on the box seat of a stage coach in the yard of the Bull and Mouth, St. Martin's-le-Grand, in the City of London. Pedlar boys offer me razors and pen knives at prices unheard of in the shops. Porters bring carpet bags and strange-

---

[8] *Pall Mall Gazette*, 10 December 1881. Edwards also issued, soon after their deaths, short biographies of the postal reformer Sir Rowland Hill (1879) and the Birmingham Liberal politician John Skirrow Wright (1880).

[9] See *Edgbastonia,* May 1886, for Edwards' account of how the magazine operated. His last contribution was in August 1889; in his final years, and after his death, his editorial duties were carried out by his son William Threlkeld Edwards.

looking packages of all sizes. There is not a lady amongst us. Coachman, guard and passengers, we are fourteen. We all wear top hats, of which five are white; each hat, white or black, has its band of black crape. William IV was lately dead and every decently dressed man in the country then wore some badge of mourning.[10]

During the whole of that long day we rattled on. Through sleepy towns and pleasant villages; past the barracks at Weedon, near which we cross a newly-built bridge, on the summit of which the coachman pulls up and we see a deep cutting through the fields on our right and a long, high embankment on the left.[11] Scores of men, and horses drawing strange-looking vehicles, are hard at work, and we are told that this is to be the London and Birmingham railway, which the coachman adds 'is going to drive us off the road'.

On we go until at length the coachman, as the sun declines to the west, points out, amid a gloomy cloud in front of us, the dim outlines of the steeples and factory chimneys of Birmingham. On still; down the wide open roadway of Deritend; past the many-gabled Old Crown House; through the only really picturesque street in Birmingham – Digbeth; up the Bull Ring, the guard merrily trolling out on his bugle; round the corner into New Street, where we pull up at the doors of the Swan. Our journey has taken us just twelve hours.[12]

And this Birmingham! The place which I, in pleasant Kent and Surrey, had so often heard of, but had never seen. This is the place which, for the first time in his life, had compelled the great Duke of Wellington to capitulate! This is the home of those who, headed by Attwood, had compelled the Duke and his army – the House of Lords – to submit and pass the memorable Reform Bill of 1832![13] My destination was at the top

---

[10] William IV died at Windsor Castle on 20 June 1837 as a result of bronchopneumonia.

[11] The barracks at Weedon, near Aylesbury, were demolished in the 1960s, though other buildings used for storing munitions survive. The first part of the London to Birmingham railway line, terminating at Boxmoor, was opened in July 1837; the section Edwards saw being constructed took the line as far as Tring and opened in October 1837.

[12] Built as a guildhall in the late fifteenth century, the Old Crown Inn was a regular venue for property auctions and, during elections, candidates met voters on its bowling green. The Swan was a coaching inn located in New Street.

[13] The Reform Bill passed the House of Commons in March 1832, but in May the House of Lords sought to remove a number of clauses. William IV asked Wellington to form an administration to secure the passage of a bill that met the wishes of the Lords, but, faced with protests in the country, the plan collapsed. Thomas Attwood in Birmingham was the figurehead of the extra-parliamentary campaign.

of Bull Street, where my apartments were ready and a walk to that spot completed an eventful day for me.

Bull Street was the principal street in Birmingham for retail business, and it contained some very excellent shops. Mr Suffield occupied premises near the bottom of the street, which he still retains.[14] Mr Adkins, the druggist, is now the oldest inhabitant of Bull Street, having been born in the house he still occupies before the commencement of the present century.[15] Mr Gargory – still hale, vigorous, and hearty, although rapidly approaching his eightieth year – tenanted the shop next below Mr Keirle, the fishmonger.[16] The Quakers' Meeting House was a long, barn-like building, standing lengthwise to the street and not having a window on that side to break the dreary expanse of brickwork.[17] Mr Benson was, in those days, as celebrated for beef and civility as he is now.[18] Mr Page had just opened the shawl shop carried on by his widow.[19] Near the coach yard was Mr Hudson, the bookseller, whose son still carries on the same business established by his father in 1821. In 1837 Mr Hudson was the publisher of a very well conducted liberal paper called the *Philanthropist*.[20] The paper only existed some four or five years. It deserved a better fate. Next door to Mr Hudson's was the shop of the father of the present Messrs. Southall.[21] All these places have been materially altered, but the wine and spirit stores of Mrs Peters at the corner of Temple Row are today, I think,

---

[14] John Suffield of 107 Bull Street sold lace, gloves and ribbons. He later expanded his business, taking over adjoining shops and augmenting his stock to include skirts, shirts and hose. He was the great-grandfather of J.R.R. Tolkien.

[15] Henry Adkins of 32 Bull Street sold drugs, which he emphasised were of the purest quality, and such other items as perfumes, vinegar, spice, and candles. In February 1869 he lost a purse, containing £7 in gold, whilst walking along Hagley Road.

[16] James Gargory of 4 Bull Street was an optician and maker of mathematical instruments. At the Exhibition of Manufactures and Arts in Birmingham in November 1849 he put on display gauges and a whistle for measuring the efficiency of steam engines of his own design. James Keirle occupied 6 Bull Street.

[17] The Quakers first occupied a site in Bull Street in 1702, demolishing and rebuilding their premises a number of times.

[18] Joseph Benson of 97 Bull Street was a confectioner and caterer, providing refreshments at public functions.

[19] Page and Grundy of 82 Bull Street advertised for 'genteel' young men to work in their shawl shop.

[20] Benjamin Hudson of 18 Bull Street established his bookshop in 1821, bringing out the *Philanthropist* on a weekly basis between 1835 and 1838 and also acting as a printer for local reformers, including Joseph Sturge.

[21] Thomas Southall was a chemist.

exactly what they were forty years ago.[22] The brothers Cadbury – a name now celebrated all over the world – were shopkeepers in Bull Street, the one as a silk merchant, the other as a tea dealer. The latter commenced in Crooked Lane the manufacture of cocoa, in which business the name is still eminent.[23] The borough bank occupied premises nearly opposite Union Passage.[24]

High Street, from Bull Street to Carr's Lane, is a good deal altered. The Tamworth Banking Company occupied a lofty building nearly opposite the bottom of Bull Street, where for a very few years they carried on business, and the premises afterwards were occupied by Mrs Syson, as a hosier's shop.[25] The other buildings on both sides were small and insignificant, and they were mostly pulled down when the Great Western Railway Company tunnelled under the street to make their line to Snow Hill.[26] Most of the courts and passages were filled with small dwelling houses and the workshops of working bookbinders. Messrs. Westley Richards and Co. had their gun factory in one of them.[27]

New Street is greatly altered. At that time it was not much more lively than Newhall Street is now. The grammar school is just as it was; the theatre, externally, is not much altered; the Hen and Chickens remains the same.[28] Hyam and Co. had just opened as a tailor's shop the queer old

---

[22] The business at 77 Bull Street was set up by Edward Peters.

[23] John Cadbury set himself up, with money from his father, as a tea dealer and coffee roaster at 93 Bull Street in 1824. His drinking chocolate business opened in Crooked Lane in 1831. Forming a partnership with his brother Benjamin in 1846, he moved in the following year to a larger shop in Bridge Street.

[24] The Birmingham Borough Company Bank - not to be confused with the Birmingham Banking Company - was established in 1837, with William Goode as manager.

[25] The Lichfield, Tamworth and Rugeley Banking Company came into existence in 1836, opening a branch in New Street before moving to premises in High Street. The manager was William Borro, but the new premises were vacated after six months when the bank failed. Mary Syson had gone within a year.

[26] The station at Snow Hill was opened in 1852. What Edwards called the tunnel was a deep cutting which for a long period lacked a roof.

[27] William Westley Richards opened what became an extremely successful business in 1812. In 1842 he invented a waterproof primer for the musket. He died in 1865.

[28] Located in New Street since 1552, the Free Grammar School occupied a new building from 1838, designed by Charles Barry; King Edward's moved to Edgbaston in 1936. The Theatre Royal opened in 1774 and was several times rebuilt; it closed in 1956. Had it been his wish, Edwards would have been able to see Charles Keen and Ellen Terry perform there during his first visit to Birmingham. The Hen and Chickens prided itself on being one of the best hotels in the town and was often used for public meetings; it was demolished in 1896.

building known as the 'Pantechnetheca' and the ever-youthful Mr Holliday was at premises converted by a now long-forgotten association called the Drapery Company; as this had not been successful Mr Holliday and his then partner, Mr Merrett, had become its successors.[29]

A few doors from this was the office of the *Birmingham Journal*, a very different paper from what it afterwards became. It had originally been started as a Tory paper by a few old fogies who used to meet at Joe Lindon's, 'Minerva', in Peck Lane and this was how it came about.[30] *The Times* had, early in 1825, in a leader, held up to well-deserved ridicule some action on the part of the Birmingham Tory Party. This gave awful and unpardonable offence, and retaliation was decided upon. Notes were sent to several frequenters of the room that, on a certain afternoon, important business would be 'on' at Lindon's and punctual attendance was requested. The room at the time was full and the table had been removed from the centre. The ordinarily clean-scrubbed floor was covered with sheet iron. A chairman was appointed and one gentleman was requested to read the obnoxious article. This over, a well-fed, prosperous-looking, fox-hunting merchant from Great Charles Street rose, and in very shaky grammar, moved that *The Times* had disgraced itself and insulted Birmingham and that it was the duty of every Birmingham man to stop its circulation in the town. This having been seconded and duly carried, another rose and proposed that in order to mark the indignation of those present, a copy of the paper containing the offensive leader be ignominiously burnt. This, too, was carried; whereupon the iron-dealer took up the doomed newspaper with a pair of tongs, placed it on the sheets of iron, and, taking a 'spill' from between the claws of the tongs, lighted it at the fire of the room and ignited the ill-fated paper, which, amid the groans and hisses of the assembled patriots, burned to ashes. This ceremony being solemnly concluded, the business began. It was deplored that the loyal party was imperfectly represented in the town. It was considered desirable that the party should have an organ in the town; and it was decided to open a subscription, there and then, to start one. The necessary capital was subscribed and a committee was formed to arrange with Mr William Hodgetts, a printer in Spiceal Street, for the production of the new paper. Mr Hodgetts subscribed to the fund to the extent of £50

---

[29] Samuel Hyam's 'Pantechnetheca' was a vast clothing shop operating from 23 New Street. His advertisements sometimes appeared in verse: 'The splendid stock in Hyam's store/Shall cause wonder from shore to shore'. Stocking the latest fashions from Paris had not saved the Drapery Company. William Holliday and his partner, at 28 New Street, were linen drapers; their shop was also the place to go for ball and evening wear.

[30] Since the eighteenth century this had been the meeting place of Birmingham's Tories. Edwards wrote about it in his *Old Taverns of Brum*, p. 12.

and the singularly inappropriate name for a weekly paper, the *Birmingham Journal*, was selected. The first number appeared June 4th 1825. The editor was Professor Bakewell. It continued in the same hands until June 1827 when Mr Hodgetts paid out the other partners and became sole proprietor. He enlarged it in 1830, at which time it was edited by the well-remembered Jonathan Crowther. In 1832 it was sold to the Liberal Party. The *Argus*, in its issue for June 1832, thus chronicles the fact:

'The *Journal* – This newspaper is now the property of Parkes, Scholefield and Redfern.[31] It was purchased by Parkes in February last for the sum of two thousand pounds and was delivered to him on the 25th of March last. Poor Jonathan was unceremoniously turned out of the editorial snuggery into the miserable berth of the editor's devil: "Oh, what a falling off is here, my countrymen!". And who, think ye, gentle readers, is now editor of the *Journal*? An ex-pedagogue, one of the Newhall Hill martyrs, a talented writer that has been within the walls etc'.

This seems to point to George Edmonds; but I cannot find any other evidence that he was ever editor. Be that as it may, Crowther remained and the paper was published at the old office in Spiceal Street as late as May 1833 when it seems to have removed to New Street and placed under the care of Mr Douglas.[32] In May of that year Mr Hodgetts published the first number of the *Birmingham Advertiser*. Meanwhile, Mr Douglas sat in the *Journal* office in New Street. It was a little room, about ten feet by six feet, and the approach was up three or four steps. Here he reigned supreme, concocted radical leaders in bad taste and questionable English, and received advertisements and money. The whole thing was in wretched plight until about the year 1844 when – Mr Michael Maher being editor – Mr Feeney, who was connected with another paper in the town, went to London, saw Mr Joseph Parkes and arranged to purchase the *Journal*.[33] Mr Jaffray soon after came from Shrewsbury to assist in the management and with care, industry and perseverance, it soon grew to be one of the best provincial newspapers in the country.[34]

---

[31] A leading figure in the Political Union, the solicitor William Redfern was essentially a Whig and closer to Scholefield and Parkes than he was to Attwood; he later became town clerk.

[32] R.K. Douglas's position as a newspaper editor made him an influential figure in the reform movement in Birmingham. He was one of the BPU leaders who addressed the great Chartist meeting in Glasgow in May 1838 and, in a party of eight Birmingham radicals, attended the Chartist Convention of 1839.

[33] J.F. Feeney, purchased the *Birmingham Journal* in 1844 before, in 1857, launching the *Birmingham Daily Post*.

[34] John Jaffray, Scottish by birth, arrived in Birmingham from Shrewsbury in 1844 to write literary pieces for the *Birmingham Journal* and was made a partner in 1852. He became the first editor of the *Birmingham Daily Post*. For Edwards' portrait of Jaffray see *Edgbastonia*, November 1885.

Mr Gottwaltz was the postmaster. A little way up Bennett's Hill was a semi-circular cove. Here was a slit into which letters were dropped and an enquiry window; and this was all. There were seven other receiving houses in the town: Mr Hewitt, Hagley Row; Mr E. Gunn, 1 Kenion Street; Mr W. Drury, 30 Lancaster Street; Mr T. Ash, Prospect Row; Mr J. White, 235 Bristol Street; Miss Davis, Lower Terrace, Sand Pits; and Mrs Wood, 172 High Street, Deritend. Two deliveries took place daily – one at 8 a.m and the other at 5 p.m. The postage of a single letter to London was nine pence, but a second piece of paper, however small, even the half of a bank note, made it a double letter, the postage of which was eighteen pence.

The town hall had been opened three years. The Paradise Street front was finished, and the two sides were complete for about three-quarters of their length; but that portion where the double rows stand and the pediment fronting Ratcliff Place had not been built. The whole of that end was then red brick. From the corner of Edmund Street a row of beggarly houses, standing on a bank some eight feet above the level of the road, reached to within a few yards of the hall itself, the space between them and the hall being enclosed by a high wall. On the other side, the houses in Paradise Street came to within about the same distance and the intervening space was carefully enclosed. The interior of the hall was lighted by some elaborate bronzed brackets, projecting from the side, between the windows. They were modelled in imitation of vegetable forms; and at the ends, curling upwards, small branches stood in a group, like the fingers of a half-opened human hand. Each of these branchlets was a gas burner, which was covered by a semi-opaque gas burner, the intent being, evidently, to suggest a cluster of growing fruits. Some of the same pattern were placed in the Church of the Saviour when it first opened, but they, as well as those at the town hall, were in a few years removed, greatly to the relief of many who thought them inexpressibly ugly.[35]

Nearly opposite the town hall was a lame attempt to convert an ugly chapel into a Grecian temple. It was a wretched architectural failure. It was the School of Medicine and, as I know from a personal visit at the time, contained a very various and most extensive collection of anatomical preparations.[36] From the town hall to Easy Row the pathway was three or

---

[35] Opened in August 1848, the Church of the Saviour was decorated with bright colours and fresh flowers and was the venue for Sunday morning and evening services conducted by George Dawson and for Saturday evening concerts.

[36] The Royal School of Medicine and Anatomy evolved from a series of lectures given by William Sands Cox in 1825. Initially based in a building in Snow Hill, it moved to the Paradise Street location described by Edwards in 1834. Its students were noted for doing well when presenting themselves for examination by the Royal College of Surgeons.

four feet higher than the road and an ugly iron fence was there to prevent passengers tumbling over. On this elevated walk stood the offices of a celebrated character, 'Old' – for I never heard him called by any other name – 'Old Spurrier', the hard, unbending lawyer who, being permanently retained by the Mint to prosecute all coiners in the district, had a busy time of it, and gained for himself a large fortune and an evil reputation.[37]

Bennett's Hill was considered to be the street of the town, architecturally. At the right-hand corner at the top there was, in a large open courtyard, a square old brick mansion, having a brick portico. A walled garden belonging to this house ran down Bennett's Hill, nearly to Waterloo Street, and an old brick summer house, which stood in the angle, was occupied by Messrs. Whateley as offices and afterwards by Mr Nathaniel Lea, the sharebroker.[38] The iron railings around St. Philip's had not been erected. There was a low fence and pleasant avenues of trees skirted the fence on the sides next Colmore Row and Temple Row. I used to like to walk there in the quiet of evening, and I loved to listen to the bells in St. Philip's church as they chimed out every three hours the merry air 'Life let us cherish'.

A few weeks before my arrival a general election took place. The Tory party in Birmingham had been indiscreet enough to contest the borough. They selected a very unlikely man to succeed – Mr A.G. Stapleton – and they failed utterly, the Liberals polling more than two to one.[39] The Conservatives had their headquarters at the Royal Hotel in Temple Row. Crowds of excited people surrounded the hotel by day and evening after evening. One night something unusual had exasperated them, and they attacked the hotel. There were no police in Birmingham then, and the mob had things pretty much their own way. Showers of heavy stones soon smashed the windows to atoms and so damaged the building as to make it necessary to erect a scaffold covering the whole frontage before the necessary repairs could be completed. When I first

---

[37] The Soho Mint was established in 1788 by Matthew Boulton. It produced mainly copper coins. In 1850 the Birmingham Mint came into operation. William Spurrier was one of the Commissioners; he lived the life of a gentleman on his estate at Heath Green, dying in 1848.

[38] J.W. and G. Whateley were solicitors. Nathaniel Lea regularly advertised his services as a man able to purchase shares in railway companies and the like in local newspapers.

[39] Augustus Granville. Stapleton had been private secretary for George Canning in the years immediately before his death in 1827. He was then awarded a government pension of £700 a year, which his opponents successfully made the issue of the election: Attwood, 2145; Scholefield, 2114; Stapleton, 1046.

saw it, it was in a wretched plight and it took many weeks to repair the damage done by the rioters.[40]

The workhouse stood about half way down Lichfield Street. It was a quaint pile, probably about 150 years old. There was a large quadrangle, three sides of which were occupied by low two-storey buildings and the fourth by a high brick wall next the street. This wall was pierced in the centre by an arch, within which the porter inside could inspect coming visitors. From this door a flagged footway crossed the quadrangle to the principal front, which was surmounted by an old fashioned clock turret. Although I was never an inmate of the establishment, I have reason to believe that other quadrangles and other buildings were in the rear. The portion vouchsafed to public inspection was mean in architectural style and apparently very inadequate in size.[41]

Aston Park was completely enclosed by a high wall. The hall was occupied by the second James Watt, son of the great engineer. He had not much engineering skill, but was a man of considerable attainments, literary and philosophical. His huge frame might be seen two or three times a week in the shop of Mr Wrightson, the bookseller, in New Street.[42] He was on very intimate terms with Lord Brougham, who frequently visited him at Aston.[43] The favourite seat of the two friends was in the temple-like summer house near the large pool in Mr Quilter's

---

[40] Stapleton invited Attwood to calm the crowd from his hotel window, but his opponent's speech antagonised his fellow Tories. Attwood was manhandled, the dragoons brought in and the Riot Act read. Accusations and counter-accusations over who was to blame for the disorder occupied the following weeks.

[41] The Lichfield Street workhouse was built in 1733. There were subsequent extensions, including an infirmary, and by the time Edwards was writing the workhouse accommodated 600 people. It was long recognised as inadequate for the growing population of Birmingham, but disputes over the site of a new workhouse delayed any action until 1850.

[42] James Watt's son was not entirely without interests in engineering: in 1817 he made the first steam crossing of the English Channel. His talents, however, lay more in business and intellectual debate. Unmarried, he died at Aston Hall in 1848. Like so many booksellers of this time, Robert Wrightson was also a printer and publisher. He brought out regular editions of the *Birmingham Directory*, listing the manufacturers, shopkeepers etc. of the town, and, in 1838, a map depicting the newly-created wards in the borough.

[43] Henry Brougham was a leading figure in Whig politics, serving as Lord Chancellor from 1830 until 1834. Distrusted by his own party, he turned to writing, embracing theology, philosophy and reminiscences. He was certainly a singular man, on one occasion faking his own death so that he could read his obituaries.

pleasure grounds.[44]   The village of Aston was as country-like as if located twenty miles from a large town. Perry Barr was a *terra incognita* to most Birmingham people. Erdington, then universally called Yarnton, was little-known, and Sutton Coldfield was a far-off pleasant spot for picnics; but, to the bulk of Birmingham people, as much unknown as if it had been in the New Forest of Hampshire.

Broad Street was skirted on both sides by private houses, each with its garden in front. Bingley House was occupied by Mr Lloyd, the banker, and the fine trees of his park overhung the wall.[45] Rice Harris lived at the house which is now the centre of the children's hospital, and the big, ugly cones of his glass factory at the back belched forth continuous clouds of black smoke.[46] Beyond the Five Ways there were no street lamps. The Hagley road had a few houses dotted here and there. The Plough and Harrow was an old-fashioned roadside public house.[47]   Calthorpe Street was pretty well filled with buildings. St. George's church was about half built.[48] The greater portion of Edgbaston was agricultural land.

The south side of Ladywood Lane, being in the Edgbaston parish, was pretty well built upon, owing to it being the nearest land to the centre of the town not burdened with town rating. Mr R.W. Winfield lived at the red brick house between what are now the Francis and Beaufort Roads.[49] Nearly opposite was a carriage way opening upon an avenue of noble elms, at the end of which was Ladywood House, standing in a park.[50] At the right hand corner of Reservoir Lane was the park and residence of Mr

---

[44]   The pleasure gardens at Aston were H.G. Quilter's lifetime's work, extending from 1818 until 1878.

[45]   After hosting the Exhibition of Manufactures and Art in 1849, Bingley House was demolished and its bricks, marble chimney pieces and staircase sold off. It was occupied at this time by Charles Lloyd, the banker and poet.

[46]   Rice William Harris, owner of the Islington glassworks in Broad Street, was appointed a Commissioner and High Bailiff. He was a teetotaller. His house is now a restaurant.

[47]   Mrs Dee presided over the Plough and Harrow at this time. During the unrest of summer 1842, the Warwickshire Yeomanry were quartered at the hotel.

[48]   St. George's was completed in 1838; Isaac Spooner was installed as its first incumbent and remained for many years.

[49]   Robert Walter Winfield was the most successful brass founder in the town. His Ladywood mansion was called the Hawthorns, and each summer his employees were invited to enjoy the grounds.

[50]   The attractions of Ladywood House, according to advertisements for tenants at this time, included a vinery and a walled garden. It was let at the time that Edwards was writing to the Misses Walker. After they left, Samuel Badge, a miller and maltster, installed himself there.

William Chance.[51] Further to the east, in Icknield Street, near the canal bridge – which was an iron one, narrow and very dangerous – was another mansion and park, occupied by Mr John Unett, Jun.[52] Still further was another very large house, where Mr Barker, the solicitor, lived.[53]

Soho Park, from Hockley Bridge for about a mile on the road to West Bromwich, was entirely walled in. The old factory of Boulton and Watt was still in operation.[54] I saw there at work the original engine that was put in by James Watt. Coming towards the town, from Hockley Bridge to the corner of Livery Street, many of the houses had a pretty bit of garden in front and were mostly inhabited by jewellers.

Coming up Livery Street, which was filled on both sides of its entire length by buildings, was the warehouse built by Boulton and Watt. Where Messrs. Billing's extensive building now stand was an old chapel built, I believe, by a congregation which moved to the large chapel in Steelhouse Lane. It was used as a chapel until about 1848 when Mr Billing bought it, pulled it down and utilised the site for his business.[55] The whole area of the Great Western railway station was covered with buildings and one, if not more, small streets ran through to Snow Hill. Monmouth Street was very narrow. Mr Thornley had a small and mean-looking shop at the corner, fronting Snow Hill.[56] At the opposite corner was a shaky-looking stuccoed house used as a draper's shop.

George Richmond Collis had recently succeeded to the business at the top of Church Street of Sir Edward Thomason.[57] It was the show manufactory of Birmingham. The buildings were a smart-looking affair. The parapet was adorned with a number of large statues: Atlas was there,

---

[51] William Chance was one of three brothers who made up Chance Brothers & Co., a large and highly-profitable glass-making business in Smethwick. The company produced glass for the conservatory at Chatsworth and later for the Crystal Palace and the Houses of Parliament.

[52] John Unett of Ickfield House lent his support to charitable causes in Birmingham, notably the General Institution for the Blind, as well as the Church Colonial Society.

[53] George Barker represented the petitioners against the incorporation of Birmingham in 1838, and also took part in the inquiry into the Bull Ring riots.

[54] Demolished soon after Edwards' visit, the Soho Manufactory had opened in 1761.

[55] According to the religious census of 1851, the Ebenezer Independent Church in Steelhouse Lane had a congregation of 570. Martin Billing ran an extensive printing business and first introduced the steam printing machine into Birmingham; he was also a paper manufacturer in Shropshire.

[56] Samuel Thornley was a chemist and grocer; he sold up in 1838.

[57] Sir Edward Thomason was a hugely successful manufacturer and exporter of medals, buttons, corkscrews and other such items in gold, silver and bronze; he sold his business to George Richmond Collis in 1835.

bending under the weight of two or three hundred pounds of Portland cement; Hercules brandished a heavy club, on which pigeons often settled; a copy of the celebrated group of the Horses of St. Mark was over the entrance. Several branches of Birmingham work were exhibited to visitors, and it was here I first saw stamping, cutting-out, press-work and coining.

There were then I think only ten churches in Birmingham. Bishop Ryder's was being built.[58] The Rev. J.C. Barrett had just come from Hull to assume his incumbency of St. Mary's; the announcement of his presentation to the living appeared in *Aris's Gazette*, October 8th 1837. I was one of his first hearers. The church had been comparatively deserted until he came, but it was soon filled to overflowing with an attentive congregation. There was an earnest tone and a poetical grace in his sermons which were fresh to Birmingham in those days. His voice was good, and his pale, thoughtful, intelligent face was very striking. He was a fascinating preacher, and he became the most popular minister in the town. The church was soon found to be too small for the crowds who wished to hear and alterations of an extensive nature were made to give greater accommodation. Mr Barrett had the peculiarity in his manner of sounding certain vowels, always pronouncing the word 'turn', for instance, as if it were written 'tarn'. I remember hearing him once preach from the text, 1 *Cor.*, iii, 23, which he announced as follows: 'The farst book of Corinthians, the third chapter and twenty-thard verse'.[59]

John Angell James was at the head of the Nonconformists of the town, and was in the prime of his intellectual powers. He was very popular as a preacher, and the chapel in Carr's Lane was always well filled. William Beaumont, the bank manager, acted as precentor, reading aloud the words of the hymns to be sung and the notices of coming religious events.[60] Mr James had a powerful voice, and an impressive manner and occasionally was very eloquent. I remember a passage which at the time struck me as being very forcible. He was deprecating the influence which the works of Byron had upon the youthful mind and, speaking of the poet,

---

[58] This church, which took its name from Henry Ryder, the bishop of Lichfield, opened in Gosta Green in 1838. It was demolished in 1960, making way for Aston University.
[59] John Casebow Barrett remained the incumbent of St. Mary's church until his death in 1881. He was regarded as the best Anglican preacher in the town. His first congregation numbered 100; in the religious census of 1851 he recorded an average evening attendance of 1500-1700.
[60] William Beaumont succeeded Paul Moon James as the manager of the Birmingham Banking Company. His financial skills were in demand in Birmingham and he offered his services as treasurer of the Society of Artists and the local branch of the London Missionary Society.

said: 'He wrote as with the pen of an archangel, dipped in the lava which issues from the bottomless pit.' Mr James was not a classical scholar; indeed he had only received a very moderate amount of instruction. He was intended by his parents for a tradesman, and in fact was apprenticed to a draper at Poole. I believe, however, that the indentures were cancelled for he became a preacher before he was twenty years of age. For myself, I always thought him an over-rated man. There was a narrowness of mind; there was a want of sympathy with the works of the great poets; and there was an intense hatred of the drama. There was, too, a dogmatic, egotistic manner, which led him always to enunciate his own thoughts as if they were absolutely true and incontrovertible. He was not a man to doubt or hesitate. He did not say 'it may be' or 'it is probable', but always 'it is'. He was a good pastor, however. During his long and useful ministerial career of more than half a century, he had but one fold and one flock. He was a firm disciplinarian; was somewhat of a clerical martinet; but his people liked him and were cheerfully obedient; and he descended to the grave full of abundant honour.[61]

Timothy East of Steelhouse Lane chapel was a man of far greater mental capacity and culture. His sermons were clear, logical, conclusive and earnest. It is not generally known that he was a voluminous writer. He was a frequent contributor to some of the best periodicals of the time. He wrote and published, under the titles of the *Evangelical Rambler* and the *Evangelical Spectator* a series of exceedingly well-written essays, the style of which will compare favourably with that of the great standard works of a century before, whose titles he had appropriated.[62]

Of the newspapers of that time, only two survive, at least in name – *Aris's Gazette* and the *Midland Counties Herald*. The latter had just been started. For a short time it was called the *Birmingham Herald*, but this was soon altered to its present title. It was published in premises in Union

---

[61] John Angell James was pastor at Carr's Lane from 1804 until his death in 1859. There were 200 members of the chapel when he took charge, but this had grown to 1500 by the time of the religious census of 1851. James was a powerful preacher, but he also extended the chapel's activities to include missionary and philanthropic work and encouraged the involvement of women. He published extensively, and his *Anxious Enquirer* (1834) ran into fifteen editions.
[62] Timothy East was a Congregationalist minister at the Ebenezer Chapel. He resigned from this position in 1843. His property was sold in 1848 and it seems he left Birmingham. The publications Edwards refers to were a series of religiously-inspired stories issued in 1823-4. East also published a number of his sermons.

Passage. It had four pages.[63] The *Birmingham Journal*, although its name is lost, survives and thrives as the *Weekly Post*. The *Birmingham Advertiser*, which on the purchase of the *Journal* by the Liberals had been started in 1833 by Mr Hodgetts in the Tory interest, was edited by Thomas Ragg.[64] It ceased to be published in 1846.

The Grand Junction railway, from Birmingham to Liverpool and Manchester, was opened on July 4th 1837 and on this line, in October of that year, I had my first railway trip in a first class carriage to Wolverhampton.[65] I returned to Birmingham by omnibus after dark the same evening, and, passing through the heart of the Black Country, made my first acquaintance with that dingy region – its lurid light, its flashing tongues of intercessant flame and its clouds of stifling, sulphurous smoke.

---

[63] Whereas the *Gazette* and the *Journal* were town papers principally concerned with events in Birmingham and its environs, the *Midland Counties Herald* sought to cover a much wider area. It came into existence as the *Birmingham Herald and Midland Counties Advertiser* in 1836, but for most of its existence operated as the *Midland Counties Herald: Birmingham and General Advertiser.*

[64] Thomas Ragg subsequently ran a bookshop in New Street as well as giving public lectures and lending his support to the early closing movement.

[65] Edwards recalled, in *Edgbastonia*, VI (September 1886), p. 135, that passengers climbed from the rails to their seats and that the floors of first-class carriages were covered with clean straw. (Second class passengers had to endure wind and rain blowing into their carriages).

Chronology

1821	Population recorded at 106,722.
1824	Public meetings in support of linking by railway Birmingham with Liverpool and with London (September and December).
1825	*Birmingham Journal* launched (June).
1828	Improvement Act gave Commissioners powers to build a town hall (May).
1830	Political Union established (January).
1831	Population recorded at 146,986.
	Huge meeting organized by Political Union on Newhall Hill (October).
1832	Building of town hall commenced (April).
	Huge meeting organized by Political Union on Newhall Hill (May).
	Botanical Gardens opened (June).
	Thomas Attwood and Joshua Scholefield returned unopposed as town's first MPs (December).
	Number of registered electors 4,000.
1834	First musical festival at town hall (October).
1835	Attwood and Scholefield returned as MPs (January).
	Market hall opened (February).
1836	General Cemetery at Key Hill opened (April).
1837	Political Union revived (April).
	Railway between Birmingham and Liverpool opened (July).
	Attwood and Scholefield returned as MPs (August)
1838	King Edward's School in New Street opened (January).
	Huge meeting organized by Political Union at Holloway Head (August).
	Railway between Birmingham and London opened (September).
	Charter of incorporation granted (October).
	First meeting of town council (December).
1839	Chartist Convention re-located from London to Birmingham (May).
	Bull Ring riots (June and July).
	Home Office control of the police force imposed by Police Act (September).
1840	First of five churches erected by the Church Building Society consecrated (October).
	Chartist Church opened with Arthur O'Neill as pastor (December).

1841	Population recorded at 182,922.
	Joshua Scholefield and George Muntz returned as MPs (August).
1842	Number of registered electors 6,129.
	30,000 signatures from the town form part of the Chartist petition (May).
	Control of police force taken on by town council (August).
	Chartist leaders George White and Arthur O'Neill arrested and subsequently imprisoned (August).
1843	Prince Albert visited 'this interesting town'. (November).
1844	Richard Spooner returned as an MP in a by-election (July).
1846	First performance of Mendelssohn's *Elijah* at musical festival in town hall (October).
1847	Muntz and William Scholefield returned (August).
1848	The Church of the Saviour, with George Dawson as its minister, opened (August).
1849	Report by Richard Rawlinson on state of public health in the town issued.
	Prince Albert visited Exhibition of Birmingham Manufactures and Arts (November).
	Prison opened at Winson Green (October).
	Public meeting adopted memorial to the Prime Minister, leading, four years later, to the foundation of the Birmingham and Midland Institute (December).
1850	Asylum opened at Winson Green (June).
	First stone of a new workhouse laid (September).
1851	Population recorded at 232,638.
	Number of registered electors 7,936.
	Abolition of the Commissioners and all powers transferred to town council (July).

The Letters

I: Public Health

Under the powers of the 1848 Public Health Act, a report was commissioned from the civil engineer Robert Rawlinson into the sanitary situation in Birmingham. Running to one hundred pages, the report, though noting that cholera was rare and that there were few cellar dwellings, drew attention to unpaved streets, confined courts, lack of drains, polluted wells and cesspools. Up until the incorporation of Birmingham in 1838, the powers of government lay solely with the Commissioners, a large body of self-appointed, wealthy men – and even after the election of the first town council that December, they continued to exercise wide powers, not being abolished until the Improvement Act of 1851. Drawing on the authority of a series of Acts of Parliament, the Commissioners did make attempts to improve the town; they had ensured the main streets were well maintained and lit by gas, levelling New Street and flagging the footpaths in 1822, and, most notably, had, in 1832-34, overseen the building of the town hall. Rawlinson's report indicated, however, that much still needed to be done, though, as the final letter in this section indicates, there was opposition on grounds of expense from ratepayers; in spite of the objections of this writer and others, the first public baths in the town were opened in May 1851.

The first letters in this section concern the cemeteries that adjoined the churches in the town centre. In the early part of the nineteenth century these were overcrowded and neglected, and it was not unknown for recently-buried bodies to be exhumed from shallow graves for medical dissection. The meeting referred to in the letter by George Goodwin led to the formation of the General Cemetery Company which, in July 1835, opened the Nonconformist cemetery at Key Hill. A Church of England cemetery was opened on an adjacent site at Warstone Lane in April 1847. Protests continued in the correspondence columns of local newspapers about the state of the churchyards in the town, particularly in relation to the spread of disease. These churchyards were finally closed for internments in February 1858.

*   *   *

Burial Grounds

Sir, The general complaint of want of a burial ground in Birmingham and the neighbourhood, especially amongst the several denominations of dissenters, has induced me to make an inquiry about the establishment of a public cemetery. I am informed that in Manchester it has been found the greatest security to the dead, and has given confidence to the friends and families of those interred. In Liverpool there is one very extensive; and, on my recently visiting it, I was much impressed by the security it gave against what are called resurrectionists, and fees much lower than in many more private burial places: eleven hundred were interred last year. In Manchester it is established by shares, and pays the shareholders handsomely, being confined to no denomination; and those who bury are allowed to have the minister of their own persuasion. A house is built at the entrance for a man and his family, who, with a watchman, patrol the ground alternately the whole of the night with dogs: a chapel is also built on the site. Surely Birmingham also ought to have a cemetery on a somewhat similar plan? A few gentlemen are anxious to establish one; and those who are favourable to such a project are requested to meet on Thursday next at Radenhurst's Hotel at twelve o'clock.
I am, sir, etc
G. Goodwin.[1]
Aris's Birmingham Gazette, 3 September 1832.

Sir, Birmingham is well known to be the most healthy of our large towns, but the salubrity of its situation is not an immunity from cholera (although, fortunately, we have hitherto escaped) and should not render us careless about the removal of positive evils. If, in the multitude of counsellors there be wisdom, we may hope that ere long our governing bodies will agree upon some comprehensive scheme which shall really promote public health, but in the meantime one important step should be taken – the graveyards in the town should be closed and closed forever. It is well known that many of these are overcrowded and that most noxious exhalations

---

[1] At a meeting at Radenhurst's Royal Hotel in New Street chaired by George Goodwin in October 1832 his proposal was adopted, with capital to be raised by the issuing of £10 shares.

arise from them, although we are happily spared the sickening and inhuman spectacles that are daily taking place in the metropolis.
I am, sir,
Your obedient servant
Z.
Sept. 15 1849
Aris's Birmingham Gazette, 17 September 1849.

Sir, In the *Birmingham Journal* this day is a letter signed 'A Constant Reader' wherein he very properly calls attention to internments in towns. He also says 'the rectors of St. Philip's and St. Martin's have closed the graveyards connected with their respective churches'. Allow me to state that, at the moment I am writing, one grave is already open in the former churchyard and two more are in the course of excavation; indeed scarcely a day passes without one or more internments immediately in front of Colmore Row. Surely, in times of disease like these, some steps ought to be taken by those in authority to prevent the continuance of a practice which is proved beyond doubt to be so injurious to public health.
I am your obedient servant
CAUTION
Aris's Birmingham Gazette, 8 October 1849.

Sir, Several of the old vaults in that part of St. Bartholomew's burying ground fronting St. Bartholomew's Row are in such bad order, as the walls are cracked and the stone nearly falling off, that there arises very disagreeable effluvia from them and which in hot weather (like we have had for the last day or two) creates such a nausea in the stomach as I think is very liable to bring on a fever; and for that reason I should feel obliged if you would insert this in your paper, that it may publicly be known, and something done towards repairing the above-mentioned vaults.
Yours respectfully,
AN INHABITANT
Birmingham Journal, 25 May 1850.

Streets

Sir, Is it not a shame – a disgrace to the town – to see the streets in the state to which they now are? Surely the rates are heavy enough to enable the Commissioners to have the streets kept a little more cleanly? Where does all the money collected for scavengers etc go to? Really, I hope this will be looked to, and the Commissioners appoint (as they ought) persons to sweep them and render them a little more decent?

I am, sir, your most obedient servant

A RATEPAYER

Birmingham Journal, 3 March 1838.

Sewers

Sir, Having been some years away from Birmingham, of which place I am a native, and having lately returned to reside here, I have been struck with the bad condition of some of the sewers which, in many of the back courts and narrow streets, are so stopped up that great quantities of filth may, in a great many places, be seen close against the doors of some of the poor inhabitants, and which must, I am sure, tend to the injury of all who are so situate. There does not appear to be a proper fall to carry off the nuisance, as may be observed by the condition of Deritend brook and the large stagnant pool at the end of Floodgate Street. If you have time and opportunity to turn your attention to the subject, and to give a little prominence to it in your valuable paper, I am sure something will be done, which must be a benefit to the town and particularly the poor.

A READER

Birmingham Journal, 25 August 1838.

Public Baths and Wash Houses

Sir – If a stranger were to visit our town and ask the very common question 'How is trade?', what other answer could he be given than this – we have two branches here busy, namely builders and gun makers. It is true that the havoc from the railway projections has done much for the former, but materially and substantially a £60,000 gaol and a £55,000 lunatic asylum have made it very satisfactory for all parties, save and except the heavily-burdened and oppressed ratepayers.[2]   The gun makers have not to complain; our own disturbed country, with the protracted continental revolutions, have created an extraordinary demand.[3] So that gaols, lunatic asylums, workhouses and guns have long taken the lead in Birmingham commercial prosperity.

But for one moment, sir, I must be serious. Now, at this depressed period, unexampled and unprecedented, I ask our public bodies, is it a time to expend, to borrow and mortgage us deeper and deeper still? I know the apathy of the ratepayers – their indifference has made Birmingham at least one of the heaviest taxed towns in England, but I cannot but raise my voice, even if it be alone, against so much inconsideration in persevering with increased rapidity and determination in adding to our local rates. £10,000 forms an item for public wash houses and baths. I will not say anything about the injudicious site fixed upon in the neighbourhood of Lower Hurst Street. Every person who thinks at all on the subject of public wash houses must know that such a neighbourhood as Thomas Street, John Street and London Prentice Street contains the only class of people at all likely to avail themselves of its advantages – if they can be considered so, or at least called for in Birmingham. I believe they are not; nor do I think they will be responded to by the class they are intended to benefit. I am not aware of any place possessing public baths and wash houses where they are erected or supported out of parish rates. I feel now, as I have ever done, at an entire loss to discover – in the absence of any reason ever having been given – why our humanity, our charity, should be coerced. I can only ask those gentlemen who have so strenuously advocated the establishment of public baths and wash houses out of parish rates would satisfy a number of dissentient ratepayers by showing that they are not doing so simply because an Act of Parliament gives them powers but that they have been incited by example or precedent.[4]

---

[2] The prison and asylum were opened at Winson Green in 1849 and 1850 respectively.

[3] Beginning in Paris in February, a series of revolutions broke out across Europe in 1848. In Britain the Chartists conscripted the support of huge numbers of working people and offered a considerable challenge to the ruling elite.

[4] In 1846 an Act was passed which gave councils the powers to build public wash houses and baths.

I am, sir,
Your obedient servant
ISAAC TROW[5]
Aris's Birmingham Gazette, 16 October 1848.

Adulteration of Food

Mr Editor, The ability and zeal which you, at all times, so willingly display in giving publicity to anything in the shape of fraud or deceit induces me to call to your attention, and that of the public generally, to a system of fraud which, I fear, is carried on to some extent by the grocers of this town: I allude to the adulteration of an article known as tea dust. Being a consumer of that article, I was struck by the singular appearance of some I purchased at an apparently respectable shop in the Bull Ring, which, upon examining, I found to contain a portion of raw sugar mixed in so an ingenious a manner as to elude casual observation. Thinking there might be a possibility of it having come there by accident, I was induced to make a second purchase, which I found to be the same. The principal consumers of this article being the industrious classes, I think it is too bad that they should be subject to the enormous tax of paying 3s 8d per lb for an article worth, in reality, only seven pence. Your making this known will, I trust, have the effect of setting the public on their guard against so barefaced an imposition, the perpetrators of which, under the garb of respectability, commit these depredations on society with impunity, while men, in humbler circumstances, whose offences, in point of cruelty and injustice, will not bear comparison, are on a daily basis banished their native land.
AN HONEST RADICAL
(We would advise the party injured to make a complaint to the magistrates, and thus bring the names of the parties before the public. This is the proper punishment – E.J.B.)
Birmingham Journal, 15 June 1839.[6]

---

[5] Isaac Trow was a regular contributor to the correspondence columns of the Birmingham newspapers. Defeated by just eighty-nine votes by Joseph Allday in St. Mary's ward in 1849, his public work was mainly concerned with the General Hospital and the Queen's Hospital. A few years before his death in 1871, this man who took such a keen interest in health and sanitary matters was summonsed for keeping a foul ashpit at his house in Balsall Heath.

II: Street Nuisances

Inhabitants of the town who were concerned about the maintenance, cleaning or lighting of the streets or the behaviour of tradesmen and other local people in them were able to write directly to the Commissioners, who might consider such complaints at their meetings; or they could write to, or visit, John Dester at the Public Office,[7] who was employed by the Commissioners to investigate such nuisances; or, as the following selection of letters demonstrates, they could seek to prompt action by a public complaint in the newspapers.

*   *   *

Dogs

Sir, I have within the last few days observed a public notice from the constables requesting, in consequence of some cases of hydrophobia having appeared in the town and neighbourhood, that persons keeping dogs would confine them, and giving notice that measures would be taken to destroy all dogs afterwards found in the streets.[8] It is lamentable to observe the disregard which is discovered to such notification by many of the inhabitants. During the present week I have seen dogs at large in the town, and much to the discredit and, I conceive, disadvantage of tradesmen, have met them on entering a shop.

I know not to what species of insensibility to trace such carelessness of human life, but, certain I am that, if it be the duty of our police to issue a notice of the kind, it is equally their duty to follow it up with utmost vigour. The inhabitants of the town will, I

---

[6] Seen a very healthy, tea was universally drunk at this time; the adulteration of the dust of tea leaves with other substances was a common practice.

[7] The Commissioners set up six committees e.g. lamp and watch and paving which met either weekly or monthly. The Public Office, in Moor Street, was in daily use as a magistrates' court and also provided accommodation for a coroner's court. The original building of 1806 was considerably extended in 1833. John Dester – whose duties extended beyond dealing with complaints about nuisances – was based there to make it easy for the Commissioners or for the inhabitants to contact him; in February 1837 his overcoat was stolen from this location.

[8] Hydrophobia was the nineteenth century term for rabies.

am convinced, justify them in adoption of the most determined measures.

I am, sir, etc

AN INHABITANT

Aris's Birmingham Gazette, 28 June 1824.

Sir, Almost every unwashed artificer you meet with either in town or country has with him his dog or dogs, and if you remonstrate with him on the impropriety of their running about in your standing grass or corn, or running after your cattle, you receive nothing but abuse. Every sporting man is obliged to pay for his greyhounds, hounds and pointers and why do not sporting men of an inferior class pay for their dogs used for bull-baiting, bear-baiting, badger-baiting, poaching etc? – for, if they can afford to keep them, they ought to be made to afford to pay for them. I deprecate and detest the brutal amusements of bull-baiting, prize-fighting, cock-fighting etc, though (shame to say) they are patronised by men who ought to set a better example; but, as these amusements do not seem to decrease, let every man who keeps his Wyndhams (alias his bull dog) or any other sort of dog be taxed for him or else be charged with the payment of poor rates.

There are other species of dogs which are exceedingly great annoyances to those unfortunate to be obliged to submit to them. I mean those little snappish, blear-eyed, bullet-eyed, flea-hunting, mangy little brutes so frequently intruded into society by many of our fair countrywomen. It is a great misery to suffer the pawings of these canine intruders (without great offence to the lady proprietor) to baste their little hides for filling your room with fleas and dirt; and there are some gentlemen so blind to the feelings of others as scarcely ever to move without two or three nuisances of this description; and, whilst you are properly engaged in business, the reptiles are moistening your door posts and claw tables and wiping their paws on your best carpet. It is high time government interfered to stop this growing evil or we shall soon have dreadful cases of hydrophobia in every town in the kingdom.

K.

Aris's Birmingham Gazette, 28 June 1830.

Sundays

Sir, I beg leave, through your medium, to call the attention of the police to a part of the town much neglected. I mean the road from Park Street to Great Barr Street, comprising Upper and Lower Fazeley Street and the walk between the pools and the canal. It is the usual route of myself and family to our place of public worship, and likewise a great thoroughfare for those going to St. Bartholomew's and other chapels in the neighbourhood. I will say nothing of the violations of public decency occasioned by so many youths bathing in the canal at a time when people are going to divine service, though this ought to be confined to places of seclusion; but I complain more of groups of blackguards and gamblers in the street playing pitch and toss and using the most revolting language, who are seen and heard there throughout the day. This very morning my wife and family were alarmed on the return from chapel by a gang of ruffians, who were encouraging two bull dogs to fight and pull each other to pieces in the middle of the street. Surely such scenes should not be allowed at any time, but particularly on a day devoted to piety and rest and sobriety of thought and action. I am sure, sir, I shall be borne out in saying that such scenes loudly call for the vigilant attention of a well-regulated police.
I am, sir,
Your obedient servant,
CIVIS
Aris's Birmingham Gazette, 14 September 1835.

Sir, Seeing in your newspaper on Saturday last, your remarks on Sunday travelling on the railway, I am happy to say that I agree with them; but I do not agree with what takes place on Sunday in this town, that is a sort of market being held in Snow Hill on Sunday morning. It often happens that a great number of cows and sheep are paraded up and down to the great annoyance of timid females on their way to various places of worship in the neighbourhood; and I have frequently seen, during the time, the street keepers have been looking on, and they have not attempted to put a stop to such disgraceful proceedings. I hope, sir, you will allow this letter to appear in your paper, as it may be a means of putting an end to such a practice. If it does not do so, I shall have recourse to those means that will compel those under whose orders the street keepers are placed to see that they do their duty.

Yours etc

G.S.

Birmingham Journal, 10 February 1838.

Sir, Permit me, through the medium of your *Journal*, to state what I consider to be a nuisance in any neighbourhood where it exists, and that I think betrays a great weakness on the part of professing Christians to support that which their consciences dictate to be wrong: I allude to the number of carriages that may be seen on any Sunday evening standing opposite Carr's Lane chapel, where scenes frequently arise from the conduct of the drivers which in my mind is calculated, if reflected upon, to call forth a blush from any person or persons in whose service they may be employed. Coming up Carr's Lane on Sunday evening last, there were no less than seven cars standing and two of the drivers of which, after using a great deal of very improper language, were just about to decide the quarrel by combat when they were prevented by the interference of the police. Hoping this may not be considered as emanating from a malevolent spirit, but that it may act as an incentive to a more careful perusal of that law which tells them to remember that they keep holy the Sabbath day.

I remain,

J.W.

Birmingham Journal, 11 August 1838.

Obstruction of the Highway

It has for a long time been a matter of surprise to me that the respectable Board of Commissioners of this town should allow or countenance an abominable nuisance in Worcester Street. I allude to the practice resorted to by furniture brokers, who obstruct the foot path, scarcely affording room for a single passenger to walk up or down the said street without subjecting themselves to inconvenience or annoyance. How frequently do we see highly respectable ladies and gentlemen prefer the middle of the street (a few inches depth of mud being no object) compared to the danger they incur by continuing on the pathway viz. by risking a fractured skull with trunks, chests, chairs, bedsteads etc which may fall by being over-weighted with other articles; or, if they escape this danger, ten to one but their cloaks, coats or dresses get torn with fenders etc; and I must say that the pathway is not over-wide, not exceeding two yards at the outside: therefore when two thirds is occupied by furniture of all descriptions, there is but a very limited space left for passengers.

Now, Mr Editor, I should like very much to know who is to blame – the furniture brokers, street keepers or the Commissioners? Let it be one party or the other who is at fault, it is certainly high time the evil was done away with, as Worcester Street is not only respectable but one of the principal through fares in Birmingham.

Your obedient servant

A POLICE RATEPAYER

Birmingham Journal, 24 February 1838.

Sir, I have observed in your paper lately several complaints made of the negligent conduct of the street keepers; but I do not think their conduct is so bad in other places as it is in Snow Hill. In that street a great number of coal carts are allowed to stand in front of the shops to the annoyance of the shopkeepers and their customers; and, when the men attending these carts are asked to remove them, insults are added to the injury done to those persons who have to pay so much money towards the support of the very men who ought to protect them and their property.

Now, sir, it may not be generally known that the Commissioners have appointed a man for the purpose of clearing the ends of Bath Street, Great Charles Street and the whole length of Snow Hill of all these obstructions to coaches, foot passengers etc. But, sir, where is the man to be found when wanted? Why in the public houses to be sure.

But, sir, I have only to add that if my fellow shopkeepers will join me in a memorial to the Commissioners, I pledge my word to present it to them (that is, if this letter does not have the desired effect), stating our complaint and asking for the dismissal from office not only of the man appointed, but of Hewson, the man that is placed over him to see that he does his duty.

Yours etc
A RATEPAYER
Birmingham Journal, 10 March 1838.

Sir, You will be rendering a great service to the inhabitants residing in Cecil Street, Newtown Row, by announcing, through the means of your journal, the dangerous practice carried on by a number of boys playing at bandy in the middle of the street, making it quite impassable. [9] I find, in the High Street, the ballad singers are considered a nuisance, and how much more is this bandy playing? Should you be the cause of removing these evils, it will be esteemed a favour by the inhabitants, and in particular your humble servant.
THEODARE BLAND
Birmingham Journal, 18 January 1840.

Lack of Lighting

Sir, You will particularly oblige a subscriber by calling the attention of the Commissioners to the state of that part of the borough called Cecil Street, which is thickly peopled and yet there is not a single light in the street, so that it is dangerous to pass through it in a dark night.
Yours respectfully
T. CUTLER
Birmingham Journal, 7 December 1839.

III: Prostitution

The very visible presence of prostitutes in the streets in the evening greatly exercised the religiously-minded, middle class men who ran the town. In the autumn of 1828 Richard Spooner, banker and former High Bailiff, and a number of prominent clergymen came together to establish a female penitentiary where young women who were venturing into prostitution could be accommodated and subjected to rules and religious instruction. Though donations and subscriptions included £60 each from the Bishop of Worcester and Lord Calthorpe as well as one guinea each from three married women from Moseley, the scheme struggled to raise funds. By the

---

[9] A game played on ice, using sticks and a ball.

summer of 1829 only £728 in donations and £277 in subscriptions had been raised, resulting in the committee of twenty men who ran the operation having to borrow £800 to purchase a building. Magdalen Asylum housed twenty women and was staffed by matrons and a residential clergyman and visited by the town's most experienced physician Dr John Johnstone. The first letter reprinted here is evidence of the reservations that existed in the town about the plan whilst the second letter seeks to bolster support for the work being done. It has been argued that the men who became involved in these campaigns were more concerned with testing their own virtue and protecting their sons than with assisting the women themselves.[10]   Certainly the third letter reprinted here offers a remarkable insight into the early Victorian male mind; for this writer the blame for the situation lies not with poverty but squarely with the morals of the women themselves.

*   *   *

Magdalen Asylum

Sir, Many well-disposed person expected that the penitentiary would be the instrument for clearing the streets of those crowds of unhappy females which nightly prowl there to the annoyance of passengers and the discredit of our police; and under this expectation they are induced to encourage the scheme. By the aid of this costly machinery it is proposed to provide servants for the rich and wives for the poor out of the class of reformed prostitutes! There is a disqualifying ignorance in these matters exceedingly becoming the character of clergymen and benevolent ladies which it would be uncharitable to deny and unprofitable to endeavour to remove. All the good which they are so kindly disposed to impart to the poor, unfortunate and penitent young female may be accomplished at least as effectually, and without any sinister operation on the public morals, by the labours of a private charity as by the *celat* and burden of a public institution. What is required in Birmingham is to have the streets cleared of that intolerable nuisance above alluded to which obtrudes itself on the public view and waylays and corrupts our young men.* This immediately

---

[10] J.R. Walkowitz, *Prostitution and Victorian Society* (1982), p. 41.

concerns our police, and if our worthy magistrates and constables would seriously and effectually direct their attention to remove it, they would confer great obligation on the community and ensure the gratitude of respectable inhabitants.

OBSERVER

*For one family who mourns over the calamity of a seduced daughter, are there not twenty families whose peace is disturbed by their sons being betrayed prematurely into vice? Would it be possible to establish a male penitentiary on the principle of the female one, managed by a committee of ladies with a visiting committee of gentlemen subject to their appointment? Perhaps by aid of a bazaar, with its attendant auctions, its raffles and its dances, the requisite funds might be raised? I drop this hint for the consideration of the lovers of novelty.

Aris's Birmingham Gazette, 22 December 1828.

Sir, I apprehend that it is not generally known that at the last annual general meeting of the Birmingham Magdalen Asylum the objectionable and limited restrictions to visit that institution were removed. Now, sir, having obtained this long desired object, I would beg leave to ask, has not this opening to our wishes honourably engaged us as a Christian society to render our prompt and effectual assistance to this house of charity and mercy? From the printed reports of the last and former annual meetings, the good which has been done and is progressively doing, is evident; for it appears that, exclusive of those placed in service, and restored and reconciled to their friends, there are not only at present twenty inmates of encouraging conduct in the asylum, but a still larger number of destitute, wretched and forlorn objects asking, or rather praying, to be admitted.

I am, sir,

Your obedient servant

Q.F.

Aris's Birmingham Gazette, 12 March 1832.

Institute for Protection of Women

Sir, I am perfectly aware that the columns of a newspaper afford but an imperfect medium for discussing a subject to which public attention has recently been drawn by a meeting of several of our townsmen most eminently useful in all that pertains to its welfare – a meeting called for the purpose of forming an Association for the Protection of Women, and for the more easy Suppression of Brothels[11]; and it is because I differ from those who think that such discussions ought not to be brought forward in the columns of a newspaper that I may be allowed to say a few words in the shortest possible space. The Society for the Protection of Women and the Suppression of Brothels must receive the warmest support and co-operation from all right-minded persons, and to a certain extent it will effect great good because its remedies and exertions will be active and it may be the means of rescuing many young and uncontaminated women from the infernal and hellish clutches of the swarms of unsexed, inhuman and fiendish procuresses and brothel-keepers who are spreading contamination far and wide amongst their own sex, making our shop men and apprentices the plunderers and pilfers of their masters' tills, ruining our gentry and filling our gaols with thieves.

My firm conviction, founded on many years' observation and experience, is that the woman is always the more blameable party; that, like a moth fluttering around the flame of a taper, she voluntarily seeks and courts her own destruction. Great evil, and a great increase of immorality, ensues from excusing the women and laying the blame to the men. I allow women no excuse; they could help themselves if they would. To them their chastity ought to be dear as life, and to be defended at any sacrifice. I am satisfied that any Society for the Protection of Women has a great deal to contend with from the general laxity of female principle. My opinions may seem ungallant, ungenerous and unmanly, but upon my conscience I believe them to be true and to know the disease is half the cure; and the truth, however unpalatable, must be spoken if useful societies are to proceed upon right principles and solid groundwork. It is a dry statistical fact that in London there are ten thousand prostitutes and in Birmingham twelve hundred, and seven hundred of the latter are the commonest strumpets; and out of this calculation are excepted all those females who are living unmarried and under protection and who justify themselves in doing so under

---

[11] Presumably inspired by the Associate Institute for Improving and Enforcing the Laws for the Protection of Women, formed in 1844. That year a bill to supress brothels failed to pass through the House of Lords.

the reasoning and deduction which naturally flows from that benignant and liberal Act of the Legislature called the Marriage Act which placed the marriage ceremony and an agreement to set a kitchen range or a copper furnace on the same easy footing by making them both
A CIVIL CONTRACT
Aris's Birmingham Gazette, 13 January 1845.

IV: Cruelty to Animals

Bull-baiting – the setting of dogs on a bull – often took place during the celebrations to mark the building of a new church. Though this activity was prohibited in the streets of Birmingham by the Improvement Act of 1773, it was not entirely suppressed - in 1798 an attempt to bait a bull in Snow Hill was broken up by militia and the final instance of bull-baiting took place at Little Hockley Pool in 1828. Graphic descriptions of bull-baiting, particularly in the Black Country, appeared regularly in the correspondence columns of the Birmingham newspapers in the 1820s and 1830s. These letter-writers objected to the brutalisation of the people as much as they did to the cruelty inflicted on the animals. Numerous parliamentary bills to abolish the practice, including in 1823 and 1825, were defeated when objections were raised that it was not a subject for legislation or that the proposed measure did not go far enough and should have also sought to make illegal fox hunting. The baiting of bulls and other animals was at last abolished in 1835. Cock fighting was not an uncommon sight in the streets of Birmingham and seemed to arouse less concern than bull-baiting – there was a public house in Deritend at this time called the Fighting Cocks. Cock-fighting was made illegal in 1849.

*   *   *

Bull Baiting

Sir, Though many years a constant reader of your paper, nothing has ever appeared in its columns gave me more satisfaction than the paragraph in last Monday's *Gazette* containing an account of the conviction of two men by your highly respected magistrate Isaac

Spooner Esq. under your new Street Act for bull baiting. [12] What, sir, must have been the feelings of any civilised being when, at the very moment of reading that account, his ears were annoyed by the savage yells of some hundreds of his degraded fellow creatures, assembled in the turnpike road, passing through this village, and engaged in this most wanton and barbarous sport?

On Monday last was held what is here termed the Wake. Who will imagine it could be very gratifying to the feelings of a Christian congregation, retiring from a place of worship, to be compelled to force their way through a crowd of bull-baiters; to see on each side of the church gates, and on the very steps, nearly a score of bull dogs held in strings, yelping with the eager desire to worry an inoffensive animal, which was quietly standing at the door of an alehouse exactly opposite the church, with a man astride its back in a state of intoxication and uttering the most profane and abominable language? This bull I after saw baited in the street.

Another case of frightful barbarity also took place. A man residing in this parish procured a large red bull and this poor beast was at intervals tied in a field in the occupation of a parishioner and was worried and dreadfully torn and lacerated by no fewer than twenty bull dogs. Driven almost to madness, the miserable animal broke the rope which confined him and ran furiously down the turnpike road leading from Dudley to Halesowen, with three or four dogs hanging to his nose and pursued by at least three hundred people of both sexes. In this manner I understand he was followed a full mile before he could again be secured and brought back to undergo fresh torments.

Let us hope that the day is not far distant when this cruel and brutalizing sport – as it is called – will be totally suppressed in law. In the meantime I doubt not the magistracy will feel it their duty to repress the practice by every method in their power; and that, as one very effective means, they will peremptorily refuse licences to those publicans who are proved to have excited and encouraged the populace to outrages so revolting to decency and humanity.

---

[12] Isaac Spooner was presented with a set of plate to mark twenty years' service as a magistrate in 1834; his younger brother Richard was later elected an MP for Birmingham.

I am sir etc
A FRIEND TO HUMANITY
Rowley Regis
Aris's Birmingham Gazette, 29 September 1828.

Sir, It must be gratifying to every friend of humanity that, during the last session of Parliament, a bill, the provisions of which, if strictly enforced, will have the effect of abolishing the horrid and demoralising practice of bull-baiting was introduced and received the royal assent. It therefore behoves the ministers and churchwardens of those parishes where the cruel system has been pursued to avail themselves of the power now placed in their hands and zealously to carry into effect the humane intentions of the framers and supporters of the bill, while every sincere friend to humanity will cheerfully lend his assistance. I shall devote my time and labour in this good cause. For want of exertion, bull baiting was carried on to a horrible extent during the last Wake at Brierley Hill, and thousands of people from distant parishes congregated together to enjoy this feast of blood. Three bulls were baited, and one to my knowledge had his tongue torn to pieces on the Saturday evening previous to the Wake Sabbath, and, for four successive days, he was torn and lacerated for their amusement in a manner too shocking to relate. Trusting that the diabolical sport will be speedily abolished.
I remain sir,
Your obedient servant,
A. SMITH
Brierley Hill
Aris's Birmingham Gazette, 12 October 1835.

Cock Fighting

Sir, Noticing a letter in your paper of Saturday last, headed 'The Streets' and signed 'An Observer', I hope you will excuse my repeating a few of his words and making one observation. Now, if this friend to 'decency and good order' had witnessed anything that was unseemly or Sabbath-breaking, and of a serious nature, the police station is so very near Camden Street that I think he might, with little trouble, have lodged his complaint in the right quarter; but, if this is too great a trouble to 'An Observer', why, in the name of 'decency and good order', could he not disperse the few women and boys that were looking on at the cocks fighting – a thing that happens so naturally in all parts of this town and is so natural to the birds themselves (when no soul sees them).

He would have run little personal risk by placing his foot between the two birds and would thus have restored 'decency and good order'; and our 'Observer' then remarks that this disgrace fell on all the bystanders. I perfectly agree with him, and merely blame him for being one of those who, sooner than exert a little personal courage or authority, will allow all the mischief to happen and then be the first to complain of it.

I am, yours respectfully,

A POLICEMAN

(Our correspondent might have gone to a magistrate, we admit. As to his interfering personally, did 'A Policeman' ever hear a proverb about a man keeping dogs and barking himself? If the inhabitants of this town are to interfere to put down indecency and disorder, they may as well save the £25,000 a year they now pay for a police – E.B.J.)

Birmingham Journal, 3 April 1841.

V: Police

Following the Bull Ring riots of July 1839, when sixty police officers from London were brought into the town, the hundred or so watchmen who patrolled the main streets were replaced by a more extensive and organised system of policing. This was done under the Police Act of 1839, in the face of opposition from the council which was due to assume responsibility for policing. Under the control of the Home Office, but paid for by a local rate, more than three hundred police constables were deployed across the town, bringing hitherto unheard of numbers before the magistrates. When, in 1842, the council took over the task of managing the police force, the number of constables was reduced to well under three hundred. This was to appease the ratepayers, who, as the following letters show, were never great admirers of their police constables.

*   *   *

Duties

Mr Editor – It really is a pitiable sight to see a policeman wandering about the streets, starved with doing nothing, this miserable weather. I suggest he might be properly and usefully employed if directed by the authorities to clear the snow from the footpaths. It would not interfere with his regular duties; and would be serviceable both to himself and his paymasters. As he has so few opportunities of displaying his willingness to give satisfaction to the inhabitants perhaps he will gladly embrace such an opportunity and be obliged by my suggestion.

PRACTICAL WISDOM

Birmingham Journal, 15 January 1842.

Sir – The utility of our police I shall not pretend to doubt – whether we have value received is a question which your contemporaries may discuss. One thing strikes me forcibly that, though a policeman may drag 'his slow length along' by the door of a ratepayer fifty times a day, he never even seems to lighten the tedium of his course by even noticing a beggar. He might prevent the most obvious imposters from troubling, in continued succession, the knockers of those who pay him, but no effort to do this seems to be made. I fancy I am as charitable as most people, for my hand is constantly in my pocket to relieve someone or other; but I think it very hard to pay the beggar, a person to open the door twenty times a day to beggars, and the policeman too; when, without force or prosecution, a threat or a slight notice or caution from the latter, would prevent many an impudent and unworthy object receiving that which I should give to one more retiring and more worthy.

Begging is a nuisance checking the flow of well-directed charitable feelings; and the attention of our most worthy, active and excellent Commissioner of Police cannot be better employed than in doing all in his power to lessen the evil.

I am, sir,

Your obedient servant

AN INHABITANT

Aris's Birmingham Gazette, 13 June 1842.

Relations with Children

Sir, Will you allow me to call the attention of your readers, and particularly that of the local authorities, to the very indecent manner in which the policemen of the town address themselves to mere children, who are, I doubt not, very tedious and annoying, particularly at this time of the year. But children will be playful; and mild, tender language should be used on all occasions, instead of the low, vulgar phrases I have too often heard used. I hope this will do something towards arresting this immoral habit, which is too prevalent amongst those who duty is to show a better example and a proper rectitude of character to those that are always imitating.
I am, respected sir,
A MORALIST
(We do not know what immorality our correspondent points at. We admit children will be playful and it is right that they should be: but we doubt the propriety of allowing them to play sliding on the pavement. Their play in that case is apt to endanger their fathers. If the policemen were guilty more constantly of the immorality of a good, sound drubbing to the playful children, by whom, in frosty weather, the necks and legs of the community are ordinarily endangered in our most public streets, they would, we think, be performing an acceptable service to most folks – E.B.J.)
Birmingham Journal, 21 January 1843.

VI: Railways

The first meetings to propose linking Birmingham by railway to other towns in Britain took place in 1824 and 1825. It was not until 1837, however, that the line between Birmingham and Liverpool came into operation, with the line between Birmingham and London opening the following year. The leading men of the town, such as Thomas Attwood and the glassmakers George Bacchus and William Chance, were great enthusiasts for the building of railways, though, as these letters show, there was also opposition. Though many businessmen and sightseers welcomed the speed of the new railways – the five hours it took to get from Birmingham to Liverpool was considerably quicker than travelling by coach - these letters show that there were also complaints about delays, fares and the standard of carriages.

* * *

Birmingham-Liverpool Railway

Sir, As a considerable holder of canal shares, I take the liberty to trouble you with a few observations on the subject of the proposed rail road from Birmingham to Liverpool; and, although I may lose more by the deprecation of the former than the profit which my more recent speculation in the latter might produce, I am not selfish enough to hope to be enriched at the expense of national welfare. I conceive, Mr Editor, that the introduction of locomotive engines may be considered a new era in the annals of this commercial country and that the formation of the projected railroad offers such important benefits to Great Britain and Ireland that it cannot be prevented by the machinations of a few interested individuals. That the canal proprietors can be absurd enough to think that an advertisement, with a few respectable names, with a lady or two and a string of unimportant persons in their train, can blind the public to the real merits of the scheme is extraordinary. I have thought it safer to take shares in the one undertaking by way of edging out the other. Is it not better to slide through a gap than 'kick against the pricks'? The premium currently offered for rail road shares (£30 for the Manchester and £7 for the Birmingham, as I am informed), and the falling prices of canal property, are sufficient evidences of the public merit of their respective merits.
I am, sir,
Your obedient servant,
DYNAMICS
Aris's Birmingham Gazette, 6 December 1824.

Sir, Allured by the high-flown picture of benefit to the public and to the proprietors so pleasingly and unblushingly drawn in the prospectus of the Birmingham and Liverpool intended rail road, I was induced to venture a few pounds in the shape of a deposit, but, the veil having been removed from my eyes, I quickly got rid of my shares. The expense of iron work and levelling the ground must, at a moderate calculation, be one million and eighty thousand pounds, being more than three times the sum of £350,000, the estimated expense of completing the main line of rail road, including the locomotive power. The £100,000 reserved for extras will not provide engines, tram waggons, and offices to say nothing of the land which will be required to be purchased, not only for the main line of rail road but also for large wharfs and coal staiths at every town near which the rail road will pass. This concern will benefit none but bankers, lawyers and surveyors.

I am, sir,

Your most obedient servant,

COMMON SENSE

Aris's Birmingham Gazette, 4 October 1824.

Sir, It is amusing to an old man like myself, who watches with some interest the results of experience, to witness the revival of the mania of 1825, with almost its original fervour. I own I am greatly surprised to find Birmingham men, either by birth or adoption, joining in and recommending a scheme to divert the great traffic which will pass on the London and Birmingham and Liverpool and Birmingham railways from coming through our town. I confess it was a great inducement to me, and no doubt to many others, to engage in those concerns that they must inevitably benefit my native town, even if should they fail to remunerate the proprietors to the extent they may expect (though on this point my hopes are very sanguine); but I trust I am one of a large number whom no prospect of profit would induce to promote a scheme which should deprive Birmingham of the advantages such noble undertakings are calculated to bring to it. I hope therefore my friends and neighbours will not (without due consideration) support the plan to which I allude, especially under the shallow pretence that at present there is no real junction between the two companies. I know that such a union has always been contemplated, and it now forms part of the plan which the Liverpool (or as it is now called) Grand Junction Railway Company are about to submit to Parliament.

I am, sir,

AN OLD FRIEND TO OLD BRUM

Aris's Birmingham Gazette, 18 November 1833.

Sir, I suggest the fancy, generally entertained, that the railroads will greatly benefit the town by introducing hosts of visitors and lots of customers is a fallacy. Posters from London to Liverpool will not now even stay to change horses or to obtain refreshment; and travellers seeking mere amusement will ever give preference to seaports and resorts of fashion. What attractions has Birmingham for this class of travellers? London and Liverpool will receive more visitors from us than they will return. The extravagant notions entertained by many respecting an increase in trade, I fear will prove equally fallacious.

BLANCO

Birmingham Journal, 19 May 1838.

Cost

Sir, On Monday the 3rd instant, having a basket, the contents of which weighed no more than 3lb, and being desirous to convey it to Coventry by the earliest stage possible, I applied at the station of the London and Birmingham Railway Company, intending to pay the carriage. I asked their charge: the reply was 1s 4d, being just 100 per cent more than the conveyance by coach for parcels of a similar description. I therefore transmitted it from the Castle coach office, the charge for which was only 8d. So much for the boasted economy of the London and Birmingham Railway Company.

AN ENEMY TO IMPOSITION

Birmingham Journal, 8 September 1838.

Sir, It is to be hoped that the attention of the public will be drawn to the very high rate charged by all existing railway companies for first class passengers. The late proceedings of the Great Western and London and Birmingham railway companies, with regard to their proposed lines to Wolverhampton, and their offer to carry goods at one penny per ton per mile, prove that the charge hitherto made by them for the conveyance of passengers is very exorbitant. I am inclined to believe that a penny per mile for each first class passenger must be more than enough if a ton of goods can be carried for one penny per mile.

I am, sir,

Your obedient servant,

VIATOR

Aris's Birmingham Gazette, 30 December 1844.

Comfort

Sir, Your appropriate remarks, some time ago, about the high fares of the London railroad met with very general approval. I have often felt surprised that the very injurious receptacles called second class carriages have not drawn forth from the animadversions of yourself or correspondents. I was therefore very pleased to see the reported observations of Mr Weston at the town council. He, however, alluded to them being made as uncomfortable as possible. That is not going near far enough: I have no doubt that many will have to date, not only loss of health, but loss of life through travelling in them. In the present month of May – I speak from experience – they are very much worse than riding outside a coach in severely cold weather. They are incomparably worse than if they were entirely open without a roof; that covering occasions such cutting currents of wind – I have not experienced rain – that the suffering is intense. They are no doubt so constructed to increase the profits of the company by inducing passengers to pay the first class fares. I know I is quite proverbial that public companies have no hearts; and this seems to settle the matter comfortably; and the individual proprietors are quite reconciled to the cold means by which their own pockets are so warmly lined.
I am, sir,
A SUFFERER
Birmingham Journal, 11 May 1839.

Railway trips

Sir, I shall feel obliged if you will give room in your next paper for the following remarks on the conduct of the Bristol railway trip on Monday last in order to put members of the public upon their guard against being misled and imposed upon in the future.

I went myself on the trip; and, in the first place, complain that instead of our being in Bristol at the time stated in the handbills, ten o'clock, we did not arrive until after one; and instead of returning to Birmingham at half past eleven, the train could not reach there until three o'clock the following morning. In the next place, the handbills stated that 'arrangements have been made for parties taking tickets for the trip to go over the largest steam boat in the world the *Great Britain* at sixpence each'. So to Bristol about six hundred and seventy of us went; and how were we treated? Why, upon producing our railway tickets and paying sixpence, we went on the vessel and were shown over part of it, but informed by persons employed for that purpose and to receive our money, that we could not see any more of it without we would submit to the imposition of paying two shillings and sixpence each in addition. Now, sir, I think the public ought to be put upon their guard against such tricks as these for, if such things are to be suffered to pass without public notice, railway trips will very soon be condemned.

I am, sir,

Your obedient servant,

WILLIAM ALLEN

Droitwich

Aris's Birmingham Gazette, 21 October 1844.

VII: Culture

Though it was pressure from the organizers of the town's very popular music festivals, which had first taken place in 1768, for a larger space to accommodate these events that persuaded the Commissioners to act, there had been a growing feeling amongst local leaders throughout the 1820s that a grand town hall would demonstrate the increasing importance of Birmingham. The Commissioners considered no less than seventy proposals, including a Greek revival building from Charles Barry, whose designs for the Manchester Institution had been accepted and who would, within a few years, secure the commission for the new Houses of Parliament. However, they opted for a submission, in the style of a Roman temple, from Joseph Hansom and Edward Welch, who had built churches in the north of England and a gaol in Anglesey. The venture was to bankrupt the two men, but, nevertheless, in October 1834, the town hall, though still unfinished, was able to host its first music festival; unfortunately, no one who attended wrote a letter to the newspapers about the event.

Of the bodies that sought to promote an interest in science and in the arts in the town, two of the most notable were the Birmingham Library and the Philosophical Society. Founded in 1779 and 1800 respectively, both had their own buildings. Over the winter, the Philosophical Society provided weekly lectures and also had its own laboratories as well as a museum and a newspaper room. As the final letter in this section indicates both bodies were, by the late 1840s, struggling to recruit support, the Birmingham Library not being helped by its high subscription rate. The call in this letter for a new body to promote educational activities in the town was to be realised with the establishment of the Birmingham and Midland Institute in 1853.

*   *   *

Town Hall

Sir,   There can be no doubt that the Commissioners who are appointed to select a design for the town hall are as desirous of proceeding upon correct principles, and of avoiding anything which may impugn their judgement and taste, as the greatest 'Sufferer from Imperfect Estimates' can possibly be; and it is no compliment paid to their suitableness for the purpose for which they are associated that your correspondent should deem it necessary to offer them instructions in what way it would be best for them to act. Does he wish the Commissioners to look upon the professional men, whom they have invited to compete together, as builders whose interest would be to mislead them; as men offering them tenders which it is their duty to scrutinize and mistrust? If I understand right, the object of the Commissioners is to select the best and most striking design which is offered for the money they have to lay out. I am sure the Commissioners will not burlesque themselves nor burlesque the country by awarding the prize where it is not justly merited.
I am, sir,
Your humble servant,
A FRIEND TO BIRMINGHAM
Aris's Birmingham Gazette, 28 February 1831.

Music Performances

Sir, From your remarks upon the splendid style in which the choruses were performed at our late musical festival, it would appear that the merit was all mine. I beg leave however to inform you that great praise is due to Mr G. Hollins (whom I am proud to boast of as being my pupil) for his skill, attention and active co-operation at the rehearsals.

I am, sir,

Your most obedient servant

THOMAS MUNDEN[13]

Aris's Birmingham Gazette, 2 October 1837.

Sir, In the *Journal* of this day, a very unwarrantable attack is made by a correspondent under the initials 'A.R.' on the Monday evening musical performances at the town hall. The public are certainly much better judges of the good musical selections and performances than the writer of the letter to which I allude, whose remarks exhibit a great want of knowledge and judgement in these matters. The full attendance at these performances may be regarded as a satisfactory test of the estimation in which they are held. I think much credit is due to the conductors of these cheap and rational amusements, and am confident the musical public will support them regardless of the unfair attack of a solitary, disaffected listener.

I am, sir,

Your obedient servant

CROCHET

Aris's Birmingham Gazette, 4 October 1847.

Philosophical Society and Library

Sir, It is impossible to avoid a sense of shame and degradation when one reflects on the literary and scientific institutions which have from time to time been established in this town. The Philosophical Institution, instituted and maintained with great success fifty years ago, has gradually dwindled into annihilation. An interesting library of scientific works not accessible elsewhere in this vicinity; a well-supplied news room; a valuable philosophical apparatus; excellent meteorological tables; good lectures on topics of sterling importance; a subscription within the means of 10,000 of

---

[13] Thomas Munden, 'Professor of Music, New Street', played an important part in organising public music performances in Birmingham, including those of his friend Felix Mendelssohn, whose oratorio 'Elijah' was rapturously received at the town hall in 1846 and 1847.

the inhabitants seemed to entitle it to the respect and consideration of the town to which, if adequately supported, it would have been an honour and a blessing, but, to which in its present state, it is a disgrace.

The Old Library, established at a still earlier period, is almost equally crippled for want of funds.[14] Notwithstanding that the population of this town has increased three fold within the last half century, notwithstanding its wealth and reputed intellectuality has increased tenfold, the number of subscribers is nearly the same as in 1800, and there is literally no demand for admission to the privileges of one of the best provincial libraries in the kingdom in one of its most populous and wealthy towns. It is a melancholy fact that this library, containing rare and curious works on all subjects, can barely obtain 550 subscribers from a population numbering 200,000.

I would suggest that a town meeting be called, and that all parties combine to raise a fund sufficient to erect on a firm basis a general Literary and Scientific Institution to be well supported with lecture rooms, philosophical apparatus, professors etc and to be further maintained by varying rates of subscription adapted to all classes. Such an Institution should not be free; for if a man will not prove his desire for knowledge by the payment of a few of the weekly pence which he spends in drink, it is useless to freely offer him what he so vilely esteems.

I am, sir,
Your obedient servant,
E.W.
Aris's Birmingham Gazette, 3 December 1849.

VIII: Religion

Though the town's leaders in the nineteenth century were drawn to a very large extent from the ranks of the Nonconformists, Birmingham was, as far as most worshippers were concerned, an Anglican town. The 1851 religious census indicated that just under

---

[14] J.A. Langford, *Birmingham: A Handbook* (n.d.), p. 69: 'The Birmingham Library, lovingly called the Old Library, originated ... in 1779; each subscriber paid a guinea entrance and six shillings per annum. Their number was so small that they could scarcely have quarrelled had they been inclined; and the whole stock might have been hid in a handkerchief'.

half of worshippers were Anglicans, with Baptists and Congregationalists accounting for twenty per cent and Unitarians four per cent. The census identified 67 churches and chapels in the town.[15] In some cases the incumbents became very well- known figures across the town. One such man was the Revd. J.C. Miller of St. Martin's (congregation: 2000), who, apart from preaching, giving lectures and bringing out volumes such as *Church of the People*, found the time to promote such bodies as the Early Closing Association and the Loan Society. Another was the spellbinding preacher George Dawson of the Church of the Saviour (congregation: 1300), who is the subject of a withering attack in one of the letters reprinted here. We begin, though, with a letter which reflects the staunch Protestantism of the 1820s as the clamour for Catholic emancipation grew; the others deal with such matters as the opening of churches in the town and charges imposed by some chapels.

*   *   *

Protestantism

Sir, Allow me to remind the Protestants of this town and neighbourhood of the obligations they are under to the Rev. Mr Burnett of Cork who, when unexpectedly called upon, stood forth the able champion of principles common to all Christians who have separated from the communion of the Church of Rome.[16]

The able manner in which he combated the dogmas and overthrew the assumed infallibility of that church must have excited the admiration and gratitude of every Protestant. Feeling myself the obligations we are under to him, and anxious that he may bear away from Birmingham some substantial testimony of the estimation in which his services are held, permit me to inform the public that the occasion of his visit to England is to obtain subscriptions to the erection of a place of worship in the city of Cork on a much more extensive scale than the present chapel. I myself have subscribed

---

[15] K. Geary ed. *The 1851 Census of Religious Worship: Church, Chapel and Meeting Place in Mid-Nineteenth Century Warwickshire* (2014), pp. 99-128.
[16] An account of the Rev. John Burnett's debate with the Rev. T.M. McDonnell at Mount Zion Chapel on Protestantism and Catholicism in August 1827 was published. His chapel in Cork was known as Mr Burnett's Meeting House.

my mite and would respectfully invite others who feel, as I do, the importance of such auxiliary aid to the cause of Protestantism and scripture truth to present him with such pecuniary assistance towards that object as their situation in life and circumstances may enable them to afford.

I am, sir,

Yours respectfully,

A CHURCHMAN

N.B. The editor has kindly consented to receive any subscriptions and to pay them over for the intended object.

Aris's Birmingham Gazette, 27 August 1827.

Access to Places of Worship

Sir, I beg leave to inquire, through the medium of your journal, what authority the governors of the Free Grammar School of this town have for giving a plot of land at Summer Hill for the purpose of building one of ten churches upon?[17]

OBSERVER

Birmingham Journal, 11 April 1840.

Sir, As it is contemplated, at a certain place of public worship in this town, to exact a certain sum of money from each person every Sunday before they enter, I shall feel obliged, sir, if you please to inform me, through the medium of your valuable *Journal*, whether by law they can enforce such an enactment?

I am, sir,

Your most obedient humble servant.

SUBSCRIBER

(We have no doubt they can. We take it for granted the place of worship is a dissenting or Catholic chapel, supported by managers, and of course their property – E.B.J.)

Birmingham Journal, 2 October 1841.

---

[17] In 1838 the Birmingham Church Building Society was founded with the aim of building ten new churches in the town. Eventually five were built, one of them, St. Stephen the Martyr being funded by the governors of King Edward's School. This church was demolished in 1950.

Sir, Being in the habit of visiting Birmingham occasionally in the pursuit of my business and esteeming it a privilege at all times to be able to attend the daily services of the Church, I am induced to remind your readers of the loss they sustain by the general practice in Birmingham of neglecting to open the churches morning and evening for daily prayer. I do not pretend to say with whom the fault rests – I point only to the fact of omission. Nevertheless I feel the loss whenever I visit Birmingham. My own church at home supplies me with 'daily bread' which I cannot get in the same way at Birmingham.

I am, sir,

Your obedient servant

A CORRESPONDENT

London.

Aris's Birmingham Gazette, 5 November 1849

George Dawson

Sir, I have long grieved to observe the conduct of a person of this town who has succeeded in drawing around him a large congregation and whose views and proceedings are calculated to produce considerable mischief. I should not, however, have obtruded upon public notice my own view regarding him had I not conceived it my duty, both to churchmen and a large body of dissenters, to raise my voice against a book he has lately published – a collection of psalms and hymns.

Some of the pieces possess considerable merit and are perfectly sound in doctrine; other are below mediocrity; and many, if not really heretical, are, at least, very doubtful. The levity with which the name of the Redeemer is mentioned, and the amount of dignity bestowed on it, judging as we may from its position in a poem by Fox, the Anti-Corn Law lecturer – one of a class of writers the editor of this collection is fond of quoting – would of itself create a serious fear that in the vital point of the Trinity all as not well.[18] There are no statements of Christian experience – of hope,

---

[18] W.J. Fox was a one-time Unitarian minister who became a paid lecturer for the Anti-Corn Law League in 1843. His domestic arrangements – he set up house with the daughter of a friend seventeen years his junior – provoked widespread criticism.

of faith, of joy, or of experimental practical religion. In spiritual hymns we need all of these phases of feeling but in the present collection we find none of them. A great fault appears to be that a large portion of the songs and hymns are totally unfit for use in the solemn worship of Almighty God. Who for a moment would tolerate the introduction of political or party songs or of love ditties into God's service? Take an instance of one of the love songs:

Life may change but it may fly not/Hope can vanish but can die not/Truth be veiled but still it burneth/Love repulsed but it returneth'

This is from Shelley, an infidel. At page 266 is an incomprehensible stanza from R.W. Emerson, another semi-infidel. Many of the miscalled hymns are mere declarations of what appears to be rapid approaches to revolution. Mr Dawson is evidently a young man who, with that particular aptitude of young men for conceit and change of opinion, has prided and plumed himself upon more than he possesses and has consequently fallen into great and grievous errors. He has indulged in glittering yet hollow speculations which every day have led him further and further from the truth into mysticism and which will speedily plunge him into positive infidelity.

I am, sir,

Yours obediently

D.

Aris's Birmingham Gazette, 4 October 1847.

IX: Politics

The absence of MPs to represent its growing commercial importance became increasingly a cause for dissatisfaction in Birmingham in the first decades of the nineteenth century. This is evident in the first letter – a mass meeting, a petition, the support of *Aris's Gazette* and great efforts from the Whig MP Charles Tennyson-D'Eyncourt had, in 1826-8, all failed to secure the transfer of the seats of the corrupt East Retford to Birmingham. The failure to do anything for Birmingham led directly to the establishment of the Political Union, under the leadership of Thomas Attwood, in January 1830. How significant the mobilization of the people through mass meetings was in the passing of the Reform Act of 1832 has been much debated by historians, but the Political Union certainly focused attention on Birmingham.[19] One supporter of reform, the button maker John Turner, made clear in a letter his unwillingness to be involved in this sort of popular politics. Other inhabitants of the town wrote letters setting out their objections to the illuminating of houses and the ringing of church bells in support of reform during the general election of May 1831.

The Political Union, dormant for several years after the passing of the Reform Act, was revived in 1837. The objective now was to secure manhood suffrage, secret voting and the payment of MPs. In the first phase of Chartism, Attwood and the other leaders of the Political Union were significant figures; at a huge meeting of 150,000 people in Glasgow in May 1838 to adopt a reform petition devised in Birmingham, Attwood was the star turn. However, Attwood and the other Birmingham men were soon eclipsed by Feargus O'Connor in the north and, though they attended the Chartist Convention in February 1839, soon withdrew from the movement, a clear indication, it has been argued, of 'a number of general problems created by the participation of an urban middle class in a radical working class movement'.[20] Though, under the leadership of George White and Arthur O'Neill, the Chartist campaign remained alive locally, the town was, after the Bull Ring riots of July 1839, no longer a bastion of support for the movement. The suppression of nightly meetings in the Bull Ring between 4 July and 15 July by sixty police officers brought in from London and by troops led to the destruction of property – and, a call, in one letter reprinted here, for something more than the two fire engines of the Birmingham Fire Office.

Of the four men who represented Birmingham in the years that immediately followed the Reform Act of 1832, the most colourful was George Frederick Muntz (1794-1857). This tall, heavily-bearded man was self-educated, very wealthy as a result of his invention of an alloy of zinc and copper and very blunt in all that he said and wrote, as indicated by his letters reprinted here. He topped the poll in the five elections he contested; he denied that he

---

[19]   C. Flick, *The Birmingham Political Union and the Movements for Reform in Britain 1830-1839* (Folkestone, 1978); N.D. LoPatin, *Political Unions, Popular Politics and the Great Reform Act of 1832* (Basingstoke, 1999).
[20]   C. Behagg, *Politics and Production in the Early Nineteenth Century* (1990), pp. 184-5.

did anything to encourage the disorder that featured in the election of 1837.[21]

*　　*　　*

Parliamentary Reform

Sir, I have watched with considerable interest the proceedings in Parliament with reference to the case of East Retford and the projected transfer of the elective franchise to Birmingham; and I recollect the general feeling of satisfaction which was called forth amongst us at the prospect acquired by the town entering into the full privileges of the constitution. I hope that on the final rejection of this part of the measure proposed by Mr Tennyson, an event now pretty certain, I shall have an opportunity of meeting my fellow townsmen and of uniting with them in some common expression of disappointment that so important a town as this should be denied the advantage of representation; and at the same time of testifying the high sense entertained here of the judicious, manly and persevering efforts of Mr Tennyson in furthering the principle of reform so temperate in its character and so well calculated by keeping up the energy of existing institutions to supersede other and visionary schemes of reform.

I am, sir, etc

AN INHABITANT

Aris's Birmingham Gazette, 14 July 1828.

Sir, Mr Attwood's memory must have failed him at the last public meeting when, with reference to a conversation held with me, he imputed to me the following observation: 'I do on my conscience solemnly believe that we are on the verge of a most tremendous convulsion'. I did say that a reform in our Commons' House of Parliament was absolutely necessary and that the voice of the nation alone would accomplish it; but I added 'that he must keep better

---

[21] Eliezer Edwards, *Personal Recollections*, pp. 79-88 depicted Muntz as an egotistical, thin-skinned, vain and knowingly eccentric man – at one meeting in 1847, he theatrically ate his way through a supply of oranges. After hearing him address a meeting, George Dawson informed Edwards, 'They won't be able to print Muntz's speech verbatim ... no printing office in the world would have capital I's enough'.

company before I could go with him', meaning thereby what he must have fully understood from the whole tenor of my remarks that the mode he was adopting for the formation of a Political Union was calculated to produce not reform but revolution.
I am, sir,
Your obedient servant
JOHN TURNER
Heath Green
Aris's Birmingham Gazette, 1 February 1830.

Sir, Am I to conclude that the chairman of the meeting on Thursday last has taken the necessary steps to ensure safety to those who may decline to illuminate their houses on Monday night at the dictum of that assembly? Or may I trust, sir, that the public authorities of the town will feel it to be their duty to extend protection to those who may not consider such a public manifestation of rejoicing called for?
I am, sir,
X.
Aris's Birmingham Gazette, 2 May 1831.

Sir, It has been asserted that on the day of the last illumination, the curate of St. Philip's applied to two of our worthy magistrates stating that he was in momentary expectation that an attack would be made on the belfry of the church for the purpose of ringing the bells (the churchwardens having, in the exercise of their undoubted right, refused to permit them to be rung) and requesting the assistance of the police to prevent the expected outrage. That, although the magistrates were perfectly aware that the Revd. Mr Moseley, the rector of St. Philip's had been pelted in the streets for refusing a similar application and that the belfry of that church had afterwards been forcibly entered and that, although the bells were at the moment of application ringing in their ears, yet they refused the assistance of a single police officer to protect St. Philip's. That an hour and a half afterwards the belfry of St. Philip's was entered by the mob and the bells rung till twelve o'clock at night. These assertions are so monstrous and incredible, that I am confident they only require to be made known to ensure their receiving unqualified denial.

I am, sir,
Your obedient servant
ALPHA
Aris's Birmingham Gazette, 16 May 1831.

Sir, I observe that there is an attempt to revive the Political Union in this town. Although I am assured the effort will be abortive when I reflect upon the injury which was inflicted upon this community for several years, a character of turbulence having attached to it, which induced strangers to take another route rather than travel through the town to the great detriment of the manufacturers and shopkeepers, I feel confidence that all proper influence will be exerted to prevent a return to the pestilent nuisance which you, sir, took so decided and creditable part in exposing in its absurd features and pretensions. I feel most deeply for the sufferings which a time of commercial difficulty entails upon the industrious classes, and it is because I believe that such an incubus as another Political Union would only increase their sufferings and prevent a return of prosperity that I would more earnestly oppose myself to so obvious an evil.
I remain, sir,
Your obedient servant,
A MANUFACTURER
Aris's Birmingham Gazette, 24 April 1837.

Bull Ring Riots

Sir, May I beg ask the magistrates whether the centre of the town is again to be made the scene of confusion? I perceive the Chartists are meeting in the Bull Ring this evening to the amount of some hundreds.
AN INHABITANT
Aris's Birmingham Gazette, 10 June 1839.

Sir, Can it be true that the Mayor of Birmingham addressed the Chartists in the Bull Ring on Thursday night and promised to use his best endeavours to obtain the use of the town hall for them to meet in? The question is important and demands an answer for the report is confidently circulated by persons who profess to have been present on the occasion to which I have referred.

A BURGESS
Aris's Birmingham Gazette, 24 June 1839.

Sir, Amongst the various arrangements made by the council for the benefit of the town, I am not aware that the formation of a fire brigade has yet engaged its attention. Regarding the extent of the borough and its rapid growth in every direction, I cannot but think that the council would act most judiciously by establishing a brigade, the men composing which could, with little difficulty, be combined with the police force. The excellent arrangements of the fire insurance companies, their promptness and liberality, upon every occasion deserve all praise; still several fires occur simultaneously and in different quarters, somewhat remote from each other, I fear that the existing force, excellent as it is, might be found inadequate to cope with the destructive element; and, after the lamentable and disgraceful outrages of last night in the Bull Ring, I am emboldened to address these hints to you for insertion in your paper, should you think them worthy of a place in your columns.
ONE OF YOUR NUMEROUS READERS
(This is a very useful suggestion, and we have no doubt the companies would give it every facility).
Birmingham Journal, 20 July 1839.

G.F. Muntz

Sir, As I never fight with shadows, I shall not answer the letter in the *Advertiser* signed 'P.Y.M.', which, I presume means 'Paltry Young Monkey', except that he will take off the blind of Toryism and then he will see that, if I know little of finance, he knows nothing about it.
G.F. MUNTZ
Birmingham Journal, 1 April 1837.

Sir, Upon returning home yesterday, after an absence of three weeks, I was astonished to see in your paper the infamous attempt to make me a party in the disturbances at the Great Hampton Street booth, upon the day of the late election, by some of the despicable wretches who do the dirty work of the Tory Party in this town. Some fellow, of the name of Woodcock, is brought forward to swear that, immediately preceding the disturbance, I rode up to the booth, took off my hat and gave three cheers, thereby intimating that I went there for the purpose of exciting the people to mischief and that I succeeded in doing so. The whole of the above is an infamous lie. I rode into town on that morning at the usual time through Great Hampton Street and passed the booth. I never pulled up my horse or spoke a word of any kind; the people cheered me and frightened my horse – I just lifted my hat in acknowledgement. The disturbance was unknown to me until after I had put my horse at Mr Parrocks, been to my mill in Water Street, remained there some time, gone to my warehouse in St. Paul's Square, opened letters, transacted the necessary business, proceeded to the booth on Newhall Street to vote, where I remained some time, returned to St. Paul's Square and passed through the churchyard into Henrietta Street, where a street keeper told me that Hall had been beating someone and the people had therefore beaten him. The above forms a fair specimen of the principles upon which the Tories here allow their underlings to endeavour to support their party cause at the expense of all they think they can injure.

G.F. MUNTZ

Birmingham Journal, 2 September 1837.

Sir, Having observed that at a meeting at Duddeston respecting a bill for lighting that district, I have been represented as having previously pledged myself to support the corporation bill, I wish to inform the public that I never did or said anything of the kind.[22] I can only say that I consider it a most objectionable bill, and one which I would never have given my support to. All that I said at the time referred to was that I would do all in my power to bring the management of the town into the hands of the corporation, which was an elective body which could always be coerced and corrected by the ratepayers if they chose to exert themselves. There seems a great desire in some quarters to connect me with the town council, in which I have never taken part and never shall belong to.

---

[22] The Duddeston and Nechells Improvement Bill, which Muntz condemned in the House of Commons as a means of protecting the positions of the Commissioners.

Yours respectfully,
G.F. MUNTZ
Aris's Birmingham Gazette, 3 March 1845.

X: A Miscellany

* * *

A False Announcement of a Marriage

Sir, In your paper of Saturday last the following was stated to having taken place, but was entirely devoid of truth:

'On the 14th instat. at Edgbaston Church, by the Rev. Mr Pixell, Mr Joseph Hickman of Warstone Lane to Miss S. Cook of Blakemore Terrace.

This is the second time my name has appeared in your paper in like manner and in both cases has been put in without my knowledge. I shall use all my endeavours to find out the party; and, if I should be so fortunate, I will do all in my power to make an example of him. I shall feel greatly obliged if you will contradict it in your paper of Saturday next, as not having taken place; by doing so, you will greatly oblige.
Your obedient servant
JOSEPH HICKMAN
(We shall be happy to give Mr Hickman every facility in tracing the impudent and stupid scoundrel who has annoyed him and imposed upon us – E.B.J.)
Birmingham Journal, 29 December 1838.

The Price of Beer

Sir, While we are blessed with cheap bread, cheap cheese and cheap butcher's meat of every description, allow me to ask why it is that ale is not equally cheap? I think the public have a right to be supplied with a good cup of ale for twopence, which, taking into consideration the present low price of malt and hops, would leave the publican a fair and reasonable profit.
Sir, yours respectfully,
A CONSTANT READER
Birmingham Journal, 8 April 1843.

The Town's Clocks

Sir, This afternoon I went with letters to the Post Office. The clock stared me full in the face and silently pointed out that the hour had just passed and that my letters were too late. The statement, however, was solemnly denied, after two minutes' consideration, by the deep tongued bell of St. Philip's, which in its turn was flatly contradicted by, after an interval of three minutes more, the clock at Christ Church expressing itself, I must say, in a very harsh and disagreeable tone.[23] Anxious to arrive at the truth, I consulted the clock at the rooms of the Philosophical Society. This clock, philosopher-like, differed from all the preceding authorities, but more nearly with the clock at St. Philip's than any other. This I thought handsome for St. Philip's is notorious for never agreeing with any other. Thus, I was, left in a horrid state of doubt, and am almost resolved to deny, with Soame Jenyns, the existence of such a thing as Time.[24]

But to be serious – it is an evil that the clocks of our various churches cannot be made to agree; but it is an even greater evil that the clock at the Post Office should be two minutes and a half in advance of the true time, as kept by Dent's excellent chronometer at the Philosophical Society's rooms in Cannon Street.

The loss of the post is a serious matter; and it is hard to be told that your letters are too late when you know you have more than two minutes to spare.

If I was an alderman (which is the highest object of my ambition), I would bring the subject before the town council; but, as I am not, I can only appeal to you for redress.

I am, sir,

Your obedient servant

CHRONOS, Jun.

Aris's Birmingham Gazette, 26 October 1846.

---

[23] J.A. Langford, *Birmingham*, pp. 90: 'It is certainly one of the ugliest churches in the town'. Christ Church, completed in 1815, was demolished in 1899.

[24] Soame Jenyns (1704-87) was a poet and essayist noted for his wit.

The Botanical Gardens

Sir, I have just read the complaint of 'A Subscriber' in the *Journal*; it is the commencement of restrictions on the shareholders depriving them of access to the Botanic Gardens before the hour of eight a.m., just the time when many of us who are employed in business were in the habit of enjoying a morning's walk, some for health and others for recreation.[25] I can scarcely think the managers can be serious for to say the least of it, it is an outrage on our just rights. I, for one, was induced to take new shares when these gentlemen found it necessary to rescind the previous ridiculous restrictions; and now, in the middle of my yearly subscription, I am prevented from enjoying my before-breakfast walk, which was one of the inducements for talking my new shares.
I remain, sir,
Yours etc
A SHAREHOLDER
Aris's Birmingham Gazette, 10 September 1849.

Sir, Why should not these Gardens to be opened at seven in the morning during the summer months and on Sundays after morning service all the year round? I pay a guinea a year; but I can seldom enjoy a subscriber's privilege of walking in the Gardens because they are always shut at such times as would suit men like myself who are 'constant at church and change'; and there are many such.
I am, sir, yours etc
A SUBSCRIBER
Aris's Birmingham Gazette, 20 May 1850.

---

[25] The Botanical Gardens were opened to the public in 1832.

Appendix: Notes to Correspondents

ineteenth century newspaper editors spoke directly to individual correspondents in a separate column, usually entitled 'To Correspondents'. Here they would answer queries – usually concerned with small items of local interest – and explain, occasionally brusquely, or, in the case of poetry, mostly with gentle humour, why an offering was being declined. Poetry, often by young working men, was frequently sent in to local newspapers, but only a fraction was ever published; it was common for the writer to be gently reminded of his literary inadequacies, sometimes by printing an extract from his attempt at verse-writing. What follows is a selection of responses to correspondents from the editors of the *Birmingham Journal.*

17 March 1826: The verses of G.T.B. are sufficiently pretty, ardent and amatory and, as it is a pity Ellen should be deprived of the pleasure of seeing poetically how he can express his affection, we advise him to send her the lines direct.

18 November 1826: Our correspondent who is 'Convinced There is Nothing like Leather' is by far too abusive and, were we to insert his observations on the parliamentary representation of the 'Stafford Snobs', we should be subject to another action for libel.[1]

24 March 1827: Mr Jones' letter in our next. Three columns of currency in one week would frighten all newspaper readers this side of the Tweed.[2]

8 September 1827: 'Loyalty and Unanimity' writes a very long letter; but about what we cannot comprehend.

6 July 1833: J.'s letter on the desecration of St. Mary's Church shall be attended to; but the truth is the children ought to have some

---

[1] The 'Stafford snobs' were shoemakers who worked for less than the agreed price; there was great bitterness towards them during the strike of autumn 1826.
[2] There was much discussion in the town in the 1820s about Thomas Attwood's ideas concerning a paper currency.

place to play and the dead ought to be buried in the environs of the town.[3]

27 September 1834: In consequence of a press of advertisements at a late hour, we are obliged to defer several communications.

12 September 1835: We have received numerous complaints of the manner in which business is conducted at our Court of Requests, amongst others a letter this week from H.S., and we intend shortly to submit to public notice observations on the constitution and practice of this court.[4]

4 March 1837: We are frequently favoured with poetical pieces which we cannot insert. We hope, when they don't appear, that their kind authors will suppose that they are for some good reason excluded. If we were to notice the fact otherwise than by our silence, it is simply because we have no wish to wound the feelings of youthful aspirants for Apollo's notice, which we know are, for the most part, truly sensitive. To these who have from time to time favoured us we may truly say that we read all they send us and always try hard to approve and we are perhaps as grieved as they can be when we find approval impossible. We are not very exigent. We do not look much for imagination; and we can dispense with judgement altogether, but some small attention to accent and sound is desirable; a little knowledge of the meaning of single words is absolutely required; and even a glimmering of their meaning in combination is not amiss. Spelling is but a small matter, only we have observed that they who have not learned their letters are seldom well acquainted with words. Our correspondents may demur to those truths, but they are truths for all that.

1 July 1837: We suppose the shops will be shut on the day of the king's funeral. It is a very foolish custom, we admit.

---

[3] Built on the northern edge of the town in 1774, St. Mary's was surrounded by a large churchyard; this was laid out as a garden several decades before the church itself was demolished in the 1920s.

[4] The Court of Requests in High Street dealt with small debtors.

10 November 1838: If a 'Subscriber' wishes the story about the policeman to be inserted, it is absolutely necessary he should give his name and address. It is impossible to give publication to grave matter-of-fact accusations upon anonymous authority.

29 June 1839: Censor's verses were not inserted because they were plainly ill-natured and we were not certain they were just.

6 July 1839: The case referred by Mr William Green does certainly seem to be very censorious; but he must be aware that, right or wrong, his letter is what the lawyers call 'a wicked and malicious lie' and would cost us a couple of hundred pounds at least if we ventured to insert it.

17 August 1839: The special constable who sneers at our independence would have done well to show his own by putting his name to his letter.

26 September 1840: R.B.J. writes with so faint ink that we are unable to decipher his manuscript.

27 March 1841: We don't know where to get the price of Swedish turnips or whether they are plentiful or scarce.

17 July 1841: C.H. must learn to laugh at the assertions of his Tory friends. It is rather too much trouble to contradict them.

21 August 1841: The length of W.H.G.'s letter has scared even us from an attempt to read it. Seventeen mortal pages and more to come? For whom does our correspondent imagine he is writing? For a race of antediluvian patriarchs who began the leading article of their journals on the first of January and finished the deaths and marriages somewhere about Christmas?

18 December 1841: We fear that J.B.'s verses would not 'give comfort to the afflicted minds of those who sustained a sad loss by the wreck of the *President*.[5]

---

[5] In March 1841 the British steamship *SS President*, with 136 passengers and crew aboard, sank in the Atlantic.

17 September 1842: If W.G. is anxious to find a hole in Mr Muntz's coat, we would advise him to use his own eyes in looking for it.

17 December 1842: We consider Mr Warrington's letter so important that we have, in preference to publishing it, sent it to the watch committee that they may make enquiries into the irregularities he complains of.[6]

17 December 1842: Joseph Lowe must learn to write more intelligibly and use more moderate language before we can publish his letter.

16 December 1843: We can rarely find space for letters sent to us on Friday and never for lengthy letters reaching us on that day. We have stated this at least a hundred times; but correspondents have short memories.

---

[6] The watch committee, made up of councillors, supervised the police force of the town.

Illustrations

'The steeples and factory chimneys of Birmingham'. The artist H.H. Horton taught drawing in Newhall Street.

The Bull Ring. On the right is the Nelson Hotel from where a coach left for London each morning at 7am; in 1834 a seat inside the coach cost 24s and a seat outside cost 12s.

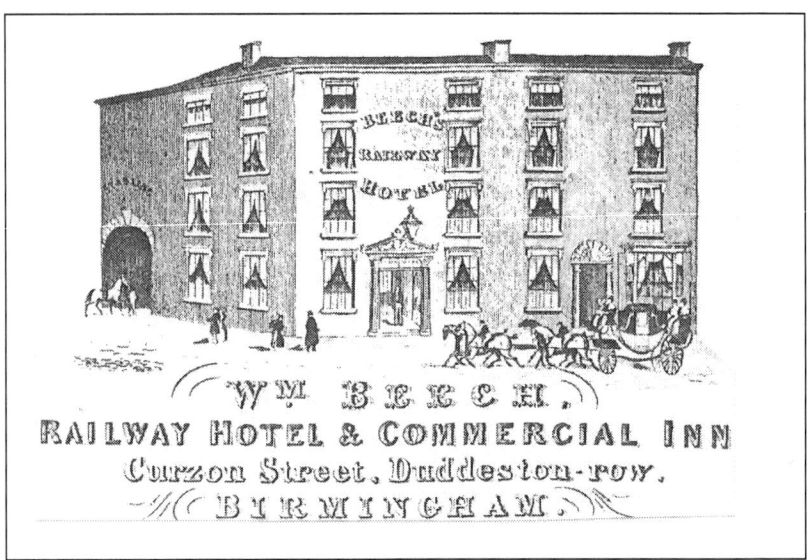

The completion of railway lines to Liverpool and London in 1837-8 led to the opening of hotels, such as that of William Beech, close to the terminus at Lawley Street. Beech died in 1843, but the hotel continued to operate.

Looking up New Street to the town hall, opened in 1834. The exhibition rooms of the Society of Artists can be seen on the right

'The excrescence called Christ Church disfigures the very finest site in the whole town'. (Eliezer Edwards). Finished in 1815, Christ Church was demolished in 1899.

Built in 1733, the workhouse in Lichfield Street provided accommodation for the poor of the town for more than a century; it was replaced by a larger workhouse in 1852.

John Showell began business as a bookseller and printer in 1829 and moved into his premises in New Street, which included a library and reading room, in 1837. He undertook to obtain a book from London 'by return of coach'.

Bull Street; at this time the most important street for shopping in Birmingham.

The great reform demonstration on Newhall Hill on 7 May 1832.
Up to 150,000 were said to have attended.

The much-admired Charles Lloyd of Bingley House, Broad Street.
The Quaker banker contributed significantly to charitable causes in
Birmingham. He was able to recite from memory lengthy sections
from the Bible, and, in his sixties, turned his attention to translating
Homer and Horace.

John Angell James of Carr's Lane Chapel; the most popular preacher in the town.

A caricature of Thomas Attwood, currency reformer and founder of the Political Union.

A caricature of G.F. Muntz, iron merchant and one of the MPs for Birmingham.

A raucous dinner for the ruling elite of Birmingham.

Bibliographical Note

I spent many hours browsing the correspondence columns of the two principal Birmingham newspapers between 1820 and 1850. I was not looking for anything in particular. My approach was simply to note down the subject matter and date of a letter if it interested me and, if it still passed muster on a second reading, to transcribe it. So this is very much a personal selection, and doubtless another historian would have selected sixty different letters. I hope, however, it will be seen a very representative sample of what was on the minds of the inhabitants of Birmingham in the first half of the nineteenth century.

The Pevsner Architectural Guide *Birmingham* by A. Foster (2005) is a superb addition to the series and has been an invaluable aid to me whilst working on this book. Also useful has been P.L. Line and A. Baggett eds. *Maps and Sketches from Georgian and Early Victorian Birmingham* (Walsall, 2013). I have regularly delved into R.K. Dent, *The Making of Birmingham* (1894); C. Gill *History of Birmingham*, I (1952); and C. Upton *A History of Birmingham* (Chichester, 1993). J.A. Langford would have been delighted to know that his *Birmingham: A Handbook for Residents and Visitors* (n.d.) has been of great use to a twenty-first century resident. Finally, I would like to draw attention to W. Dargue's excellent website - ahistoryofbirminghamchurches.jimdo.com

Index

About the Author

Stephen Roberts is Honorary Lecturer at the Research School of Humanities and the Arts in the Australian National University. Prior to this, he was, for many years, a Fellow at the University of Birmingham. He has written extensively about the Chartists, most recently as editor of *The Dignity of Chartism: Essays by Dorothy Thompson* (Verso, 2015).

THE BIRMINGHAM BIOGRAPHIES SERIES

Already published:

Dr J.A. Langford 1823-1903: A Self-Taught Working Man and the Sale of American Degrees in Victorian Britain. 65 pp, 8 photographs, 2014. ISBN: 978 1495475122. £5.99.

Sir Benjamin Stone 1838-1914: Photographer, Traveller and Politician. 102 pp, 20 photographs, 2014. ISBN: 978 1499265521. £7.99.

Mocking Men of Power: Comic Art in Birmingham 1861-1914. 60 cartoons, 2014. ISBN: 978 1502764560. £8.99. (with Roger Ward)

Sir Richard Tangye 1833-1906: A Cornish Entrepreneur in Victorian Birmingham. 65 pp, 2015. ISBN: 978-1512207910. £4.99

Joseph Chamberlain's Highbury: A Very Public Private House, 44 pp, 2015, ISBN: 978-1515044680. £3.99.

These books can be ordered from Amazon and other booksellers.

Printed in Great Britain
by Amazon